THE IMMEDIATE AFTERMATH OF WORLD WAR II

Rebuilding Nations, Redrawing Borders, and the Birth of a New World Order

Alexander L. Sheppard

TABLE OF CONTENTS

INTRODUCTION

In the summer of 1945, the leaders of the Allied nations of the United States, Great Britain, and the Soviet Union were looking for ways to finally bring an end to the destruction and chaos that the Second World War had wrought upon the world since 1939. Benito Mussolini's fascist Italy had been conquered, Adolf Hitler's German Nazi Reich had surrendered, and the Empire of Japan had stood alone in defiance against the Democratic powers for months. The core islands that comprised Japan (known simply as the "home islands") had been bombed regularly for quite some time, and the Japanese government believed an invasion of their country was inevitable and imminent. In the face of devastating daytime raids and scathing nighttime fire bombings, Japanese authorities, including Yoshijiro Umezu, the Chief of the Imperial Japanese Army, still refused to consider surrender. This would soon change. On August 5, 1945, the American military was preparing to unleash an attack on the Japanese home islands, the power of which the world had not yet seen or even thought possible.

In the early hours of August 6, 1945, the United States Army Air Force 509th Composite Group (commonly known as 509th CG) was outfitting a selection of B-29 "Superfortress" bomber planes stationed on the Pacific island of Tinian to carry out yet another bombing mission over the home islands. The target was somewhere in southern Japan, possibly on the island of Kyushu or perhaps the southern portion of Honshu, the largest of the four main islands. The exact target, however, was still unknown. In fact, one of the pilots of the B-29s, a US Army Air Force (USAAF) Colonel named Paul Tibbets, wouldn't make a final decision about the target until he and his crew were already airborne. The mission was so important, and the cargo was so precious that they couldn't risk wasting it on a suboptimal target. Recon planes were to be sent out alongside Tibbets' craft to record weather conditions over several Japanese cities to help the crew determine where their strike would work best. The selected city could have no more than 30% cloud coverage over their skies, preferably less, and the winds needed to be calm enough to reliably drop their payload without it being pushed off course by a strong gust. The USAAF also arranged for numerous other bombers to take flight on missions at the same time, just to divert attention away from Tibbets and his craft, which he had named the *Enola Gay*. For the men present that day, this would be the most important mission they would ever take part in. Tibbets took the time to brief his men on the mission and their goal, leaving out a few key details about the nature of the new and terrifying weapon they were going to be carrying. At 2:45 a.m. local Tinian time, it was wheels up. The *Enola Gay* took to the skies.

Aboard Tibbets' Superfortress was a small crew, most of whom he had hand-selected himself. Among them were Captain Theodore van Kirk and Major Thomas Ferebee. Also aboard was William Parsons, a US Navy captain and member of a secretive military technological organization that was known as "The Manhattan Project." If anyone aboard was unsure about the role of Parsons or the clandestine Manhattan Project, they would find out in just a few short hours as they flew over the skies of Japan. The crew of the *Enola Gay* was kept relatively small on purpose. The guns were unmanned, save for the tailgun, and no one except those deemed vital for the mission was included in the crew so as to keep the weight of the B-29 as light as possible. The weapon loaded onto Tibbets' plane back at the Tinian base weighed nearly 10,000 pounds, and unnecessary weight could prevent the ship from reaching the required speed and altitude. Tibbets' began climbing the ship as soon as they took off and continued the ascent on their way to American-occupied Iwo Jima, about halfway between Tinian and Japan.

Just before 6 a.m. Tinian time, the *Enola Gay* reached Iwo Jima and continued on its way. With no weather issues along the way, the mission looked promising. About an hour and a half later, the crew members had enough confidence to finally arm the massive weapon in the plane's bomb bay. Some 40 minutes later, the weather reports came into Tibbets, indicating that all three targets looked promising. It was now time to decide which city he and his crew were going to annihilate. The options included Kokura, Nagasaki, and Hiroshima. Tibbets chose the latter, and the fate of the city of Hiroshima, nestled in the deltas of south Honshu with a population of nearly 300,000 souls, was sealed. The weapon that was painstakingly loaded into the *Enola Gay* was an explosive device, but it was a bomb, unlike any of the other hundreds of thousands of bombs that had been dropped since the war began in 1939. It's nickname was Little Boy; it was loaded with uranium-235 fission material, and it was going to be the first nuclear weapon ever used in the course of war. The ensuing explosion would change the meaning of warfare forever and define the climate of global politics for the next four and a half decades.

Hiroshima was an important industrial city for the Japanese war effort. Factories there produced steel, heavy weapons and artillery, and vital components for the Imperial Japanese Army Air Service planes. The military presence in the city was also considerable, with over 40,000 Imperial Army troops stationed there. Though the population of the city had dropped markedly since the United States began its bombing campaign of the country, there were still hundreds of thousands of Japanese civilians going about their daily lives there in August 1945. When their air raid sirens began blaring through the city, warning its people to seek shelter, none of the citizens or soldiers could possibly have comprehended what was headed their way. In fact, not even the men who designed the atomic weapon fully understood its capabilities. They could estimate the explosive power of the shockwave it would produce and the scorching heat that would likely be enough to instantly melt or vaporize anything within its radius, but still, very little was known about the nature of nuclear weapons or the horrific after-effects of the radiation they released. The engineers and scientists who developed Little Boy weren't even sure if the *Enola Gay* would survive the initial blast. According to their best estimates, Tibbets needed to be at least 28,000 feet above the blast to prevent the destruction of the B-29, but all they could do was speculate.

Knowing that the armed bomb he was carrying had the potential to both wipe out countless innocent lives and end the Second World War in a moment, Tibbets approached the Japanese home island of Shikoku, south of the target, at around 7:40 a.m. local Hiroshima time.

The *Enola Gay* was still ascending. They needed to be flying higher and faster before the bomb could be dropped. After reaching the main island of Honshu, the *Enola Gay* steered sharply westward toward Hiroshima. By 8:12 a.m., the crew was flying over 31,000 feet above the city. The crew eagerly searched for the Aioi Bridge, which spanned Hiroshima's Ota River. The bizarrely T-shaped bridge was one of the most easily recognized sights that could be seen from that altitude, so they had decided to aim for that. A few minutes had passed, and the armed nuclear weapon was soon passing over its destination. The crew equipped their protective goggles to shield their eyes from the coming blast of light. Major Ferebee got everything in order, and at 8:15, it was a bomb away. The *Enola Gay* immediately jerked upwards at the release of the nearly 5-ton bomb, and Tibbets quickly swerved away in the direction of Iwo Jima, putting as much distance between his crew and the bomb as possible before detonation. Little Boy spiraled downward toward the city, and exactly 43 seconds after it dropped from the bomb bay doors, it detonated just under 1,900 feet above ground level.

First, a piercing flash of light cut across the sky of Hiroshima. Everything directly underneath the detonation zone, including the Shima Hospital, which Little Boy was headed straight for, was instantly incinerated. Tens of thousands of lives were lost in an instant. The initial shockwave leveled most structures within the radius of the blast, and those that were left still standing were soon engulfed in a fiery tornado as ground-level temperatures at Hiroshima spiked by thousands of degrees Celsius in less than a second. Somewhere between 60,000 and 80,000 people, civilian and military, were swallowed up and killed either by the blast, the fire, or the intense radiation that spread across the city and into the sky as the mushroom cloud that bloomed over the city could be seen hundreds of miles away. Tens of thousands more civilians were severely injured by the shockwave and firestorm. Later, heavy radioactive rains drenched the city and poisoned its earth. Sergeant George R. Caron, the tail gunner for the *Enola Gay*, could clearly see the blast as the crew sped away from the home islands, and to him, it was like taking a "peep into hell" (quoted in Chun, 2008). This blast, with a force roughly equivalent to 15,000 *tons* of TNT, was a defining moment in history, and a new horror had been fully unleashed. U.S. President Harry S. Truman himself hinted at the start of a new and terrifying period of warfare: "With this bomb, we have now added a new and revolutionary increase in destruction... to our armed forces. In their present form, these bombs are now in production, and even more powerful forms are in development" (6 August 1945, National Archives). There, in the once-clear skies above Hiroshima, the Atomic Age was born.

Little Boy's detonation over Japan was not the last mass tragedy of the Second World War, and it certainly wasn't the first. The war, which had touched virtually every corner of the world, had introduced humanity to destruction and calamity on an unprecedented scale. Major cities across the world were nearly wiped off the map over the six long years of conflict. Using only conventional bombs, about half of Tokyo was destroyed by 1945 due to the American bombing campaign. Roughly 80% of Manila, the capital city of the Philippines, lay in ruin. Vienna, the Austrian capital, was only slightly better off. The Chinese had lost millions of acres of arable land after the Japanese caused mass floods. The German cities of Cologne and Hamburg, today home to over 1 million Germans each, were virtually annihilated completely, with no functioning infrastructure or industry to speak of. The great city of Berlin, which Adolf Hitler had planned to transform into the greatest towering marble-clad metropolis in the world, had been left as a heap of smoldering rubble.

With all this destruction, human tragedy was inevitable. In total, estimates of the death toll of World War II range up to 60 million worldwide. Another roughly 60 million people were left displaced and homeless. Eastern Europe and East Asia bore the brunt of the human toll, with the Soviet Union alone suffering around 25 million casualties as they pushed the Nazis out of Russia and back into Germany. The Chinese lost about half that amount to the brutal Japanese Imperials. Western Europe was not left untouched, however. In Germany, the majority of the population had lost their homes. Millions of Germans were now trying to survive on the streets, and millions more were left aimlessly wandering the German countryside without even a city to return to. Deadly food shortages in Asia and Europe quickly ravaged what cities were left standing. The famine that struck Japan even before the war ended eventually cost Tokyo over 100,000 of its citizens. Beginning in 1946, the Soviet famine took the lives of hundreds of thousands more, and the Ukrainian SSR suffered particularly harshly (Grada, 2019). The nations of Europe could barely grow enough food to feed their own people, much less export food to other hungry people. Shortages of oil and fuel, the majority of which began while the war was still raging, persisted for years afterward. In some cases, the shortages of vital goods actually got worse in the post-war years. On top of this, millions of soldiers across the world were now desperately trying to reintegrate into fractured and broken societies as civilians.

The shortage of goods was a symptom of a much larger problem— entire economies across the globe had utterly collapsed, and most of the world's governments had gone into crushing debt just to fund the war effort (importantly, the vast majority of the new debt was held by the United States of America). On both sides of the war, European countries had almost completely depleted their reserves of gold to keep their militaries afloat, and governments severely debased their currencies to the point of hyperinflation. By 1948, three years after the war officially ended, prices for necessary commodities remained astronomically high. In Austria, the average price of household products had tripled, which was merciful compared to the hardest-hit economies. In France, prices had increased by 1,800% from their pre-war cost, and in Japan, by a whopping 10,000% (International Monetary Fund, IMF.org). The franc (French currency) had been debased so critically that cash was essentially worthless. It was even worse in post-war Germany, where the modern system of money exchange had virtually collapsed. People stopped using German marks altogether and instead reverted back centuries to a system of trade and barter. After 1945, the American dollar was the *only* global currency that stood tall and formidable in the face of global economic disaster.

Even the former powerhouse of the British Empire was struck by the post-war crisis. Prior to the outbreak of war in 1939, the British government was the number one global lender to countries across the world. Post-1945, they became the number one borrower. After enduring the calamity of the German bombing campaign known as The Blitz, Britain's great cities were in shambles and needed to be rebuilt, with no money or infrastructure with which to rebuild them. The nation had lost nearly half a million of its people, and most of the civilian casualties were in the capital city of London, which was the target of German bombers for months on a nearly daily basis. Britain was borrowing massively from the United States and even from their own dominion of Canada, two of the only participating countries in the world that were left almost completely intact after the war, owing to their geographical distance from the conflict. If the grim situation in Europe was to be cured, something drastic needed to happen. Most of their governments were too poor and had barely enough resources to help their own people, so there was no hope of them being able to assist their neighbors. As we'll see, the responsibility of the European recovery will soon fall on the broad shoulders of the supercharged American industry.

Countries like Britain, France, Germany, Italy, Belgium, and others that had large colonial holdings across the world could no longer afford to maintain their vast overseas empires. In regions across Asia, Africa, and the Middle East, these colonial European overlords faced new economic and social problems as their former subjects began to test the limits of colonial governance. The destruction and bankruptcy of the European continent had set the stage for the decades-long era of decolonization, a process that only further weakened the might and prestige of the world's former powers. The nations of Western Europe that had long exerted their influence on every corner of the earth had now fallen by the wayside and were supplanted by just two new global superpowers. They were the only two nations left that still had the strength, resources, and influence necessary to be able to determine the course of international politics—the United States and the Union of Soviet Socialist Republics (USSR), commonly known as the Soviet Union.

The massive demand for American industrial output during the war had catapulted the nation from being a mid-tier regional power to being the most influential, rich, and powerful nation in the world, aided by the fact that aside from the bombing of Hawai'i in late 1941, the United States remained untouched by the horrors of bombing raids. With their factories producing like never before, the American economy was primed to dominate the world's markets. American post-war power was rivaled only by the Soviet Union, a nation that had developed massively despite being one of the biggest victims of German aggression. These two ideologically opposed superpowers, once allies in the fight against Nazism, have since come to challenge one another for political dominance. With the old powers of Europe having to largely abandon their global empires, ambitions, and roles on the world stage, the way was cleared for the USA and the USSR to prepare to expand their influence and ideology across the Americas, Europe, and beyond. The Americans and their western allies sought to establish a new world order based on the principles of democratic freedoms and capitalist economies, while the Soviets envisioned an ever-growing global socialist community with the USSR (and more specifically, Soviet leader Josef Stalin) as its unquestioned and unchallengeable leader. These two visions for the world were fundamentally incompatible, and the stage had been set for the new Cold War, one fought with espionage, propaganda, subversion, and proxy rather than guns and ships. At the heart of this new political division between the East and West lay the weapon and technology that was displayed with deadly effect in Japan in August 1945—the atomic bomb, the weapon that would remain at the forefront of the minds of every political leader, regardless of alliance or allegiance, for the next 45 years.

The first nuclear detonation in human history, named "Trinity," took place on July 16, 1945, in a controlled setting at a New Mexico testing site. The second in history took place in Hiroshima, the first ever used in the course of war. Incredibly, even the immense destruction of the Little Boy bomb wasn't enough to force an immediate Japanese surrender. That was accomplished with the third nuclear detonation in history. But why were weapons of this magnitude even necessary to win the Second World War, a conflict in which all of Japan's allies had already surrendered unconditionally? Simply put, the concept of surrendering instead of fighting to the death was unthinkable by the majority of Japan's military and government, from the politicians to the foot soldiers. When it became obvious to the Japanese that an invasion of their home islands was likely, they began conscripting millions upon millions of Japanese civilians, including women and children, and training them to defend Japan with sharpened sticks, crude clubs, and spears made of bamboo. Further complicating matters was the fact that the Japanese Empire had barely enough material to clothe their standing army soldiers, which meant that outfitting the militia in uniforms was out of the question. The possibility of distinguishing hostile soldiers from innocent civilians was going to be impossible, meaning that a traditional American invasion of Japan would result in unbearable casualties on both sides. An intelligence officer in the Fifth Air Force named Colonel Harry Cunningham took note of the intense mustering of civilian militias throughout Japan, famously remarking, "The entire population of Japan is a proper military target... there are no civilians in Japan" (Malik, 2020).

Estimates of the total American death count from the planned invasion ranged up to 1 million. America's leaders began to consider the terrible power of nuclear weapons as a convenient way to avoid losing so many young American lives. Many others who were in favor of the bomb option were concerned with the state of the world that they foresaw once the war was over. The bipolar post-war world came as a shock to nearly no one when it emerged between 1946 and 1948. The Soviet Union had long been an imperial power, by nature seeking to dominate its neighbors and spread the ideology of communism. By 1945, Stalin and Field Marshall Georgy Zhukov had amassed such a massive standing army and had advanced so much in technological power that they were in a position to be able to march right across Europe. If they had simply kept marching after they had pushed into the German heartland, there would not have been a single European power strong enough to stand up to the full might of the Red Army. In the east, the Soviets were also making worrying gains across Asia. If the United States could demonstrate to the entire world that they now possessed the power to level entire cities, it would serve as a warning to the Soviets, preventing them from steamrolling across the continent.

Many American leaders had moral reservations about using atomic weapons in actual combat, including Generals Eisenhower and MacArthur, but President Truman ultimately determined that it was the only course of action to prevent continued war and intolerable loss of American life. Three days later, when Little Boy did not result in an immediate Japanese surrender, the Americans dropped yet another nuclear weapon, named Fat Man, on the city of Nagasaki, southwest of Hiroshima. If given enough time, it is likely that Japan would have surrendered after Hiroshima, but the Americans had a point to make. They needed to convince the world that Hiroshima was not an isolated event and that the Americans had an unknown, possibly limitless supply of city-annihilating atomic weapons. Fat Man, a hefty and round bomb powered by radioactive plutonium 239, was significantly more devastating than the uranium-powered Little Boy. Both bombs were used on cities that had remained relatively unscathed by the conventional American bombing campaigns, specifically to demonstrate exactly how powerful they were. Shockingly, many Japanese military officials *still* advised against surrender and insisted on continuing to train and enlist civilians in the armed forces. Ultimately, though, Japanese Emperor Hirohito made the final decision to accept unconditional surrender. The two nuclear weapons proved effective, and the United States emerged as the victor of the Pacific War, ushering in a new era of war and fear.

A photograph of the massive nuclear explosion over Nagasaki.

The open conflict and violence of the Second World War had ended in defeat for the Axis powers of Germany, Italy, and Japan. Not everything was quite yet settled, however. The atrocities of the war had been so terrible that a simple surrender was not enough to please anyone. The Holocaust, engineered by the German Reich, had claimed the lives of millions of innocent Jews, other racial minorities, and disabled people by the middle of 1945. In the east, the Imperial Japanese Army had changed the meaning of suffering for the millions of innocent Chinese who lay in the path of their westward conquest. The horrors of the First World War shook the world, but this was different—here, the brutal and calculated murder of innocent civilians was a main objective of the war, not an unfortunate byproduct. From top-level generals to foot soldiers, the cruelty of combatants was unlike anything the world had yet seen, and so retribution was in order. The question on the minds of every European leader was what exactly to do with Germany, a nation that, in the space of just a few decades, had waged two massive wars against all of their neighbors. Some European leaders wanted to completely disarm the German people, potentially permanently, to prevent them from ever going to war again. Others wanted to forcibly destroy *all* German infrastructure and manufacturing capability and reduce Germany to a nation of subsistence farmers. Others, mainly the Americans, saw Germany as a potentially powerful ally in the coming conflict against Soviet communism. They wanted to rebuild Germany with liberal, democratic values and eliminate the desire for Germany to go to war in the first place. The ultimate fate of Germany is a central subject of this book.

When the dust had settled, and with the past seemingly behind them, the new leaders of the free world sought to ensure that Europe would never again be brought to the brink of destruction. In late 1945, the victorious allies created the United Nations (UN), a spiritual successor to the failed League of Nations that was created in the wake of the First World War. This new international body was to be the supreme arbiter between disputes among the great powers of the world and would ensure peaceful resolutions to conflict. At least, that was the hope. The initial major signatories of the UN Charter included the USA, the UK, France, China (who at the time was embroiled in a bloody civil war), and the Soviet Union. The United Nations was partially a successful endeavor, but the threat of an all-out nuclear war was never too far-fetched in the post-war years, and besides that, tensions only rose in the immediate aftermath of the war between the UN's chief members. The dropping of the first nuclear weapon and the rise of the USA and USSR as global superpowers defined the next era, but before the tragic chapter of world history that was written between 1939 and 1945 could be put to rest, the men responsible for it had to be brought to justice. Indeed, the first months and years after the surrender of the German and Japanese Empires were consumed by revenge. Throughout these chapters, we will take a look at the state of the world that these same men left in their wake.

CHAPTER 1:
CRIMES AGAINST HUMANITY—NUREMBERG, TOKYO, AND THE HOLOCAUST

When peace was established in 1945, the world had begun to heal from the wounds of the Holocaust and the mass slaughter in the East. But what was to be done about the Axis leaders themselves, the men responsible for perpetrating these modern horrors? There was a lot of disagreement among the victors as to what their fate should be. Some believed they should be hunted down and executed without trial. Some were indifferent. In the end, these men, many of whom are among the greatest villains of the twentieth century, took the stand in international court and were tried as war criminals. Both in Germany and Japan, the top surviving military and political brass of the Axis were brought before the world to establish their guilt. In the end, some were executed, some were imprisoned, but many received hardly any punishment at all. In the case of Nazi Germany, many of their leaders either committed suicide alongside Adolf Hitler or were able to escape Europe altogether with the help of friendly governments and the Vatican in Rome, never seeing any kind of judgment for their deeds. Some of the luckiest among them were even recruited into the ranks of their former enemies. How the world dealt with the aftermath of the world's greatest atrocities between 1945 and 1946 remains highly controversial.

The Concept of Genocide

In 1944 and 1945, as the Allied armies of the United States, Britain, and the USSR pushed inward from the east and west across German-occupied territory, they began encountering the machinery of the Holocaust. They were the concentration camps, also known as death camps, where Europe's Jews had been held captive, enslaved, and murdered. Leaders of the Allied nations had suspected, and in some cases were aware of, a large German operation to systematically eradicate the global Jewish population. Many of the soldiers who first happened in the camps, however, had no idea what they were about to witness. They were prepared to find prisoners of war unduly executed, but what they found instead were mass graves, train cars overflowing with dead and decomposing bodies, heaps of discarded jewelry, and piles of shoes that belonged to the millions of victims of the Holocaust. Worse still, they found legions of survivors so badly malnourished that they resembled walking corpses more than anything else. The first of the camps was liberated in the summer of 1944 by the westward-bound Soviet Red Army marching through Poland. Its name was Majdanek, and the horrors it concealed within its walls quickly earned it the nickname "the Cemetary of Europe."

On January 27, 1945, the Soviets liberated another camp, Auschwitz-Birkenau, now the most infamous of all the camps. One Red Army soldier who was present at Auschwitz when it was captured later recalled what he had seen: "We saw emaciated, tortured, impoverished people... We could tell from their eyes that they were happy to be saved from this hell" (quoted in Tharoor, 2015). In the coming months, many more similarly disgusting camps were discovered and liberated by the Soviet, American, British, and Canadian armies. There are tens of thousands of bodies lying in piles, on trains, and on the backs of trucks. Evidence was discovered that suggested that, in fact, millions of lives had been brutally cut short in these camps. Gas chambers equipped with false showers that fed a deadly gas known as Zyklon B were also discovered, suggesting that the murders had been planned and carefully executed for years. The scale of human misery and death shook the liberating soldiers, who were now responsible for taking care of what survivors had left. Soldiers broke down, crying, as dying Jews rushed to greet them as heroes and saviors. In later years, and with much research, it was discovered that between 1933 and 1945, over 6 million of Europe's Jews had been murdered by the Nazi regime.

The world needed to know what had happened in the camps. People across the world, particularly in Europe and North America, had long been aware that German Jews were being persecuted, publicly branded, and discriminated against, but few could have imagined what was happening behind the curtain. They would have to see it with their own eyes. Allied soldiers and officers began diligently collecting and recording as much evidence of the crimes as they could—photographs, records, and other physical evidence. This evidence was subsequently published in America and elsewhere, bringing light to the Holocaust. It was also kept for use later when the men responsible would be brought forth in judgment. The liberating armies took it a step further when they began forcibly marching German civilians through the camps to show them exactly what their beloved Nazi government had committed.

After the liberation of the camps, even with all the evidence they had gathered and the timeline they had pieced together, Allied leaders and soldiers were at a loss for describing what they witnessed inside the camps—quite literally, in fact, as there was not yet a word to describe the crimes they discovered. The intentional attempt at extinguishing an entire race of people was more than murder, and it was certainly more than "casualties of war." So what was it? In 1944, a Jewish Polish lawyer named Raphael Lempkin coined the term "genocide," meaning the intentional extermination of an ethnic group, to describe such things, but it had not yet become a popular term. After the war, Lempkin, who was lucky enough to have escaped to the United States when his native Poland fell to Hitler, was determined to make "genocide" an official, recognized term and to establish it as a separate crime under international law. In 1945, Lempkin was allowed to attend the Nuremberg Trials, in which the top surviving Nazi brass were prosecuted. His efforts paid off to a degree, and for the first time, the term "genocide" was heard on the world stage as it was included in the list of indictments against the Nazis. However, Lempkin wanted the perpetrators to be charged specifically for committing genocide, which was impossible since it was not yet considered an actual crime. Nuremberg only strengthened his resolve, however—while there, he discovered that nearly 50 of his relatives were murdered during the Holocaust.

After the trials, Lempkin continued to lobby intensely for genocide to be considered not only a crime but a crime against humanity, another term that was popularized as a direct result of the Holocaust and the subsequent trials at Nuremberg. Simply put, Lempkin argued that such targeted violence against racial groups was not only a crime against the victims of the violence themselves but against the basic human decency of people everywhere. It was an assault on humanity. After the creation of the UN, he lobbied there as well, and in 1948, they finally approved the Convention on the Prevention and Punishment of Genocide, which unambiguously criminalized targeted violence against entire ethnic groups. The Holocaust was neither the first nor the last instance of ethnic violence in human history, but it was a pivotal moment in the world's understanding of murder on a grand scale. Since 1945, the Holocaust has functioned as the yardstick against which other genocides are measured, and targeted racial attacks are often compared to it. Even the term "Holocaust" has been frequently borrowed to describe acts of ethnic violence, including those that predated the Second World War. The genocide against Armenians in the Ottoman Empire that began in 1915 had started to be called the Armenian Holocaust, and the term was also used to describe the Rwandan genocide against the Tutsis in the 1990s.

The Holocaust was a sobering moment in history, but in reality, it was only the latest in a long line of atrocities against Jews. Having been subject to expulsions and brutal pogroms for centuries, the Holocaust was more of a culmination of high levels of anti-Semitism within Europe. As a result of their historic persecution, many Jews began to support the ideology of Zionism, essentially the idea that the global Jewish population needed a homeland of their own, preferably in the Middle Eastern region of the Levant, the birthplace of Judaism and the historic home of the Kingdoms of Israel and Judah. After the Holocaust, support for Zionism, which was already on the rise, skyrocketed. Both Jews and non-Jews had been convinced that the establishment of a Jewish nation-state was not only justified but also a moral imperative. Especially in the US and the UK, the latter of which had actively dedicated themselves to the Jewish cause, many leaders were now in agreement that fostering a country for the world's Jews in the Levant was a wise decision. Unfortunately, the land that this new nation was meant to be built upon was also home to groups of Arabs who had lived and raised their children on that land for generations. In recent decades, these people have come to see themselves not just as Arabs but as distinctly ethnically Palestinian, and they are also eager for a nation of their own. The groundwork had been laid for one of the most significant ethnic conflicts of the 20th and 21st centuries. Before any of this could unfold, however, justice for the millions of victims of the war needed to be handed down.

1945: The Nuremberg Trials

There were several disagreements over how best to punish the German leaders who had subjected Europe's Jews to the gas chambers and who brought an entire continent to the brink of ruin. This issue needed to be dealt with tactfully—the last time Germany was punished for their warmongering was after the First World War, and the resulting Treaty of Versailles served as the foundation for Adolf Hitler's rise to power. The Soviets, for one, wanted a show trial. This was a classic concept in the Soviet legal system, where the guilt of the accused is predetermined, usually without much evidence, and a phony mock "trial" is held to give the illusion of fairness, impartiality, and due process. Many British leaders went a step further. They called for summary executions of the surviving Nazi leaders, i.e., they wanted no trial at all, preferring simply to round up the men they believed to be guilty and execute them extrajudicially. However, the Americans, specifically President Harry Truman, lobbied for an actual and legitimate international criminal trial in order to showcase the superiority of the American "way" and to demonstrate his confidence and conviction in the American legal system. He sought to prove that even with a fair court hearing and defense lawyers, the Nazis would be found guilty of their crimes and brought to justice. Due to the fact that the US was the only non-communist nation powerful enough to throw its weight around post-World War II, Truman eventually got his way. Just months after the fall of the German Reich, the new world order, with America as the central, influential powerhouse, had begun to take shape. Few decisions were going to take place without the nod of approval from the Americans.

The first task was to choose a site for the historic trial. The Allied leaders finally settled on the German city of Nuremberg for a number of reasons. It was the most practical choice—there were going to be a lot of representatives present from the various countries involved, and Nuremberg was home to one of the few large courthouses in Germany that had not been completely destroyed by Allied bombs. It also had a lot of symbolic significance. Nuremberg was one of the main cities in which the toxic ideology of Nazism grew, and from here, it spread outward through other German cities. For years, the grandest Nazi Party rallies were held in Nuremberg with fantastic turnout and celebration. It was the city where Nazi officials announced the 1935 racial policies, also known as the "Nuremberg Laws," which outlined persecutory restrictions on Jews in the nation and barred marriage and sexual intercourse between Jews and so-called "pure-blooded" Germans. Now, the Allies wanted to turn "one of the chief spiritual homes of Nazism" (Glees, 1992) into the city where Nazism officially died.

On August 8, 1945, just two days after the Japanese city of Nagasaki was bombed, the Allies were already setting the trial in motion. That day, they issued the London Charter of the International Military Tribunal, which confirmed their intention to legally prosecute and punish those responsible for the six years of destruction. It also established a number of legal concepts that would be used to charge the defendants, who included Hermann Goring, the infamous leader of the German *Luftwaffe*; Field Marshal Alfred Jodl; Hitler's Deputy Rudolf Hess; and Karl Donitz, the man who served briefly as the leader of the German Reich following Hitler's suicide. The first of these charges was crimes against peace, referring to the waging of an aggressive and unprovoked offensive war. Second, were war crimes, i.e., breaking well-established rules of conduct in war, including mistreatment of prisoners of war and execution of those who had surrendered, both of which the Germans (and, for that matter, the Americans, British, and Soviets) were guilty of. The third concept was crimes against humanity, referring to the wholesale murder and attempted execution of entire ethnic groups. The inclusion of this third concept is largely thanks to the efforts of Raphael Lempkin.

The main portion of the trial, the Major War Criminals' Trial, took place between November 1945 and October 1946 in Nuremberg's aptly named Palace of Justice. The international judges set to try the Nazi leaders had a heavy weight on their shoulders. As American

Justice Robert H. Jackson said in his opening statement, "the wrongs which we seek to condemn and punish have been so calculated, so malignant, and so devastating that civilization cannot tolerate their being ignored because it cannot survive their being repeated... what makes this inquest significant is that these prisoners represent sinister influences that will lurk in the world long after their bodies have returned to dust" (Trial of the Major War Criminals, 1945). Brought to trial were some of the most fundamental engineers of the war and the Holocaust, but in total, only 24 individuals were meant to be tried. Many of the highest-ranking Nazis, those closest to the Fuhrer, had committed suicide before the war had even concluded, including Joseph Goebbels, the man in charge of Nazi propaganda, Heinrich Himmler, in charge of the infamous paramilitary *Schutzstaffel* or "SS," and Adolf Hitler himself. Martin Bormann was listed among the 24 defendants at Nuremberg, as the Allies were unaware that he also took his own life prior to Germany's surrender.

Considering the lasting mark that the war had left on the world, the total of 24 defendants, of whom only 21 actually appeared in court, seems inadequate. This is especially shocking considering that the racist and ultranationalist Nazi ideology was not confined to a small, elite group of Nazi politicians, ideologues, and generals. It was, in fact, widespread through German society and institutions, and far more were complicit in the Holocaust than the Allies initially believed. With time, the world came to understand how many individuals took part in these crimes and "that far broader groupings, including the German Army, participated in the process of genocide" (Glees, 1992). Indeed, many average German soldiers ran wild through the towns as they conquered and slaughtered the Jewish populations. SS units, which typically followed behind the *Wehrmacht* (German armed forces), cleaned up the rest and systematically went through population records to identify Jewish citizens. Still, 24 men apparently carried the cross for all of them. Of these, only ten received death for their actions. A total of 12 death sentences were handed down, but one of them was Martin Bormann, who was already dead, and another was Heinrich Himmler, who had died by his own hand the night before he was scheduled to be hanged. Three men were found not guilty for their actions. The rest were simply given prison sentences of varying lengths. Was justice truly served?

In later months and years, subsequent trials were held by individual nations in Nuremberg that targeted specific groups of people and institutions. One was held to try the lawyers and judges of the German Reich, the men behind the notorious German race laws that subjugated Jews and other groups, like the Romani people and the disabled. One of these men was Wilhelm Stuckart, one of the co-authors of the Nuremberg Laws. Stuckart, however, was one of the ones that got off easy. His sentence was "time served," meaning that his time in captivity before his trial was deemed sufficient. He was released and lived his life as a free man until 1953. Another trial was held specifically for Reich medical personnel, referred to as the Doctors' Trial. Its aim was to prosecute the doctors behind the horrific medical experimentation that was done on Jewish prisoners within the concentration camps, particularly on women and children. These experiments, which the Nazis considered to be on the bleeding edge of medical science, were cruel and horrifyingly sadistic.

Another trial was held specifically for German industrialists and corporations that either profited from or directly participated in the war effort and the atrocities of the Holocaust. These companies benefited greatly from slave labor provided by Jewish prisoners, and they included IG Farben, a massive German chemical conglomerate that used Jewish slaves for their workforce. The Allied nations later forced IG Farben to break up into numerous smaller companies, as they had grown so large that they wielded significant political power in the former Reich. Two of the companies that formed as a result of IG Farben's breakup were Bayer and BASF, two large companies that are still active today and that had a significant role in manufacturing Zyklon B, the pesticide that was used to kill Jewish prisoners.

The subsequent trials set a precedent for the legality of wartime behavior—subordinates in the military could no longer be excused for their crimes by using the excuse that they were "only following orders." Individuals were still responsible for the moral consequences of their actions, regardless of whether they were being instructed by a superior. Even before the Holocaust began in full, soldiers were being commanded to massacre Jewish and Romani civilians, but if the excuse of "following orders" was legitimate, everyone would be able to pass the buck all the way up to Adolf Hitler. The line had to be drawn, and to this day, soldiers are expected to refuse direct orders that violate moral principles or that constitute war crimes.

Still, somewhere in the neighborhood, 185 individuals were brought forward in the various trials that happened after the Major War Criminals' Trial. Of these, only 12 received the maximum penalty of death. Another 85 received varying prison sentences, many of which were later reduced. Many of the Nazis went on to live full lives after their sentences, and the question of whether Nuremberg actually achieved justice for the millions of lives taken by the German war machine remains a subject of debate even today. Still, there is no question that the Nuremberg process was an important step in establishing international criminal law and the concept of crimes against humanity. It was also the catalyst for the UN's Universal Declaration of Human Rights in 1948, which established inalienable safeguards for the freedom and lives of all people, regardless of ethnicity, religion, or gender. These moral advancements were characteristic of the post-WWII world.

1946: The Tokyo Trial

The crimes of the Second World War were not limited to Europe, and the suffering endured by the peoples of East Asia at the hands of the Japanese rivaled that of the Eastern Europeans. In the name of fascism and global expansion, the Japanese were particularly brutal toward the Chinese. Like Nazism, Japanese fascist ideology was also racially supremacist—the Japanese viewed themselves as one of the world's premier Asian races and believed they were destined to control and exert influence over the rest of the continent. They pursued this goal with deadly effect. In early September of 1945, just days after the Japanese Emperor Hirohito agreed to surrender and ordered his armies to cease combat, American General Douglas MacArthur, the supreme commander of Allied troops in the Pacific theater, ordered the immediate arrest of dozens of Japan's top military and political leaders. This included General Hideki Tojo, the Japanese commander-in-chief for the majority of the war.

MacArthur ordered that the prisoners be held in preparation for a trial that would mimic the monumental Nuremberg trials. These proceedings lasted quite a bit longer than Nuremberg, beginning in 1946 and not handing down final sentences until 1948. It was officially referred to as the International Military Tribunal for the Far East, or IMTFE, and it included several prosecutorial nations, including the USA, the USSR, France, the UK, and Canada. It also involved nations whose homes were directly threatened by the Japanese, including India, China, the Netherlands (who had colonial holdings in the Pacific that Japan assaulted), and Australia, whose people were, for quite some time, in constant fear of invasion. The day after the Japanese attacked the United States at Pearl Harbor, Hawai'i, Australian Prime Minister John Curtin made a desperate plea: "Men and women of Australia, the stern truth is that Japan has commenced a war in the Pacific in which our security and our vital interests are at stake. I ask the people of Australia to do the best that they can in service to this country. The fighting forces are at battle stations... this is the gravest hour of our history" (Digest of Decisions and Announcements No. 10, 1941). The next year, the fear was even more intense, and Curtin told his people that "the protection of this country is no longer that of a contribution to a world at war but the resistance to an enemy threatening to invade our own shore" (Digest of Decisions and Announcements No. 19, 1942). Though the Japanese had already canceled their potential plans for an invasion of Australia, the swift conquest of their neighbors continued to terrify them.

The Tokyo Trial began on April 29, 1946, almost exactly one year after Adolf Hitler took his own life. It saw 28 defendants tried—the top brass of Japan's military and government. Notably, however, not a single member of the Japanese Royal Family was put on trial in Tokyo. In fact, they were able to retain their prominent positions in Japanese society, which was a vital condition of Japan's surrender in the war. They were, however, reduced to symbolic figurehead positions, even more so than they were during the war. A total of seven of these defendants were sentenced to death, and these included Prime Minister Hirota Koki and the former top General Hideki Tojo. It was lucky that Tojo was actually able to be tried in the first place. When American troops surrounded his home on September 11, 1945, Tojo grabbed a pistol and attempted to commit suicide by shooting himself in the heart. The Americans found him slumped over in a chair, barely clinging to life, but the general had missed his heart completely and was able to be resuscitated. The very next day, the Japanese Field Marshal and notorious butcher of China, Hajime Sugiyama, did not have such poor aim. He unloaded four rounds from his pistol into his chest, destroying his heart and leaving him bleeding out. Tojo would have to wait a bit longer before his life could end. He admitted responsibility for the war, but even as he was recovering from his attempted suicide, he refused to admit wrongdoing, claiming that "the Greater East Asian War was justified and righteous... I would not like to be judged before a conqueror's court. I wait for the righteous judgment of history" (Toland, 2003). In late 1948, after judgments were handed down, Tojo was hanged.

Like Nuremberg, several subsequent trials were held that targeted "lesser" war criminals, including politicians, industry magnates, and even soldiers. Many of them were given life sentences, but several were released on parole after only a few years in prison, and from 1947 to 1948, Douglas MacArthur released dozens who had not yet even faced trial. In later years, when Americans relinquished military control over the Japanese home islands, Japanese officials released even more of those sentenced in the Tokyo Trials. One of these men was Shigetaro Shimada, the supreme commander of the Japanese Imperial

Navy, who received full parole from his life sentence in 1955. Also, in keeping with the precedents set by Nuremberg, the prosecutors in the Tokyo Trials also tried to dismantle and dissolve the massive Japanese industry conglomerates that either benefited from the war or provided the Japanese military with the tools and weapons they used to wage the war. These conglomerates were referred to in Japan as *zaibatsus*, and like the German IG Farben, they commanded significant political power in the country. The effort was only partially successful, however.

The *zaibatsus*, which included such modern-day companies as Mitsubishi and Nissan, were fundamental to the national economy and were generally believed to have been beneficial to industry despite their monopolization of various sectors. American leaders soon grew hesitant about the idea of crippling the Japanese economy in such a way because, even as they were tying up the loose ends of WWII, they were preparing for the next global conflict that they saw on the horizon. It was the goal of the Allies to establish Japan as a strong counterweight to the growing threat of communism in Asia. The USSR's eastern frontier neighbored Korea and China, the latter of which was currently embroiled in a communist revolution of its own. Japan, it was hoped, would become a democratic and staunchly capitalist nation, which could only be accomplished if Japan's industry remained powerful. So, the dissolution of the *zaibatsus* was done half-heartedly by the Americans, who soon became completely opposed to the idea. One of the largest *zaibatsus* was Mitsubishi, which fabricated the dreaded Mitsubishi A6M "Zero" fighter planes that were used to terrify the American Navy with suicidal *kamikaze* attacks during the war. Mitsubishi was forced to disorganize into separate companies, but this lasted only until the early 1950s when the Korean War broke out.

Then, fear of communism drove the Americans to allow Mitsubishi's free reign to remerge into the massive international corporation that it remains today.

Although the successes of all these trials were incomplete at best, both Nuremberg and Tokyo were important precursors to international criminal law, which continued to develop over the following decades. They set precedents for perpetrators of war crimes and crimes against humanity, precedents that would guide global reactions to atrocities in the foreseeable future. By the end of 1948, both Nuremberg and Tokyo had concluded. The world was a very different place, but perhaps now it could at least begin to heal from the wounds of the Second World War, despite the fact that countless perpetrators of the Holocaust were able to be successfully funneled out of Germany in the wake of their surrender, including Adolf Eichmann, one of the most important so-called "architects" of the Holocaust. Eichmann, like many others, was able to escape to Argentina through the "rat lines" under the name Ricardo Klement with the help of Nazi-sympathizing Catholic Bishops like Alois Hudal. Eichmann, however, would meet justice soon enough at the hands of Israeli special agents. For the time being, though, it seemed as though enough discipline had been doled out. Unfortunately for everyone, the world was now on the brink of a new and terrifying chapter in human history, one dominated by fear and anxiety over the new type of weapon that the USA demonstrated over the skies of Hiroshima and Nagasaki. Worse, Europe was still a ways away from being a functioning society again. It needed to be rebuilt.

CHAPTER 2:
THE NEW EUROPE

After the Second World War, Nazism and fascism were no longer widely appealing political philosophies in Europe. Adolf Hitler and Italian dictator Benito Mussolini, two of the most voracious and enthusiastic fascist ideologues on the continent, were both dead. The effects of unrestrained and violent ultranationalism had been felt deeply in every aspect of European society and life, and the victorious nations were keen to prevent it from ever taking root again. The last real bastion of fascism in Europe now lay in Spain, where Francisco Franco's isolated dictatorship stubbornly clung to fascist militarism for several more decades. In every other nation, the social order was in flux. However, it was not just European politics and alliances that shifted post-1945, but the economic landscape and the very geography of the continent. Borders were being redrawn, nations were being rebuilt, and the hands of new, powerful players were guiding the process. Europe needed help.

Rebuilding: The Marshall and Molotov Plans

After the successful detonations of the Little Boy and Fat Man nuclear bombs, the Western nations no longer had to fear the Soviet war machine continuing to rumble across Europe. With the knowledge that the Americans possessed such a weapon, Soviet military expansion would be kept in check, at least for the most part. Yet the threat of a communist takeover remained. European economies were struggling terribly, and American and British leadership were acutely aware of the fact that internal communist groups might rise up throughout Europe, overthrow the old democratic systems, and align politically and economically with the Soviet Union. Their fears were justified— generally speaking, support for communist forms of government was strongest during times of hardship and economic uncertainty. Many Western leaders, notably British wartime Prime Minister Churchill, viewed Soviet communism as potentially an even greater threat to Europe than Nazi Germany. Churchill had always taken a harder line against communism than he did against Nazism, and he was particularly adamant in the years after WWII that Josef Stalin had to be swiftly dealt with. Privately, he considered that the Americans should even use their new nuclear weapons against the Russians before Stalin could become strong enough to challenge them: "We ought to not wait until Russia is ready... fifty-two percent of Russia's motor industry is in Moscow and could be wiped out with a single bomb. It might mean wiping out three million people, but they [the Soviets] would think nothing of that" (quoted in Kitchen, 1987). He and many other Western leaders were as determined to prevent Soviet gains as they were to reverse German ones.

In order to hasten the recovery of devastated European countries and to bolster the potential targets of Soviet infiltration, American President Truman and his Secretary of State George C. Marshall developed the European Recovery Plan, commonly referred to as the Marshall Plan, after its chief advocate. Its primary goal was to ensure that the former nations of Europe could be secured as strong, democratic allies for the coming conflict against the Soviet Union. This was to be achieved primarily through large cash injections into the local economies, which were initially a point of contention as Truman's enemies in Congress didn't like the idea of funneling millions out of the USA and into foreign nations. Something would have to be taken in return. However, Truman and Marshall were adamant about the necessity of the plan. At the graduation ceremony for the Harvard class of 1947, George Marshall used his opportunity to speak to introduce the Marshall Plan to the public and to make his case for why it was in the best interest of the entire world:

> The feverish preparation for war and the more feverish maintenance of the war effort engulfed all aspects of national economies. Machinery has fallen into disrepair or is entirely obsolete. Under the arbitrary and destructive Nazi rule, virtually every possible enterprise was geared into the German war machine. . .thus a very serious situation is rapidly developing which bodes no good for the world. . .the consequences to the economy of the United States should be apparent to all. It is logical that the United States should do whatever it is able to do to assist in the return of normal economic health in the world, without which there can be no political stability and no assured peace (Remarks by the Secretary of State at Harvard University on June 5, 1947).

The aid that the United States had committed to sending to Europe took the form of vital foodstuffs, which were severely lacking on the continent, various important industrial goods like fuel and machinery components, and, most importantly, cash investments. Over the length of the plan, the United States had injected a total of over 13 billion US dollars into various European economies, the equivalent of close to 100 billion USD in 2020. Great Britain, the island nation that had been torn apart by the German air raids and rocket attacks, was by far the largest recipient of funds released under the Marshall Plan. Truman and the American Congress believed that Britain needed to return to its pre-war industrial production rates if they were going to be able to serve as America's primary ally against the USSR in Europe. The British Isles received a little over 25% of all Marshall Plan funds directly.

Without question, suggesting the Marshall Plan at all was a risky move for Truman. He had approved it right before making his bid for reelection, and conservative Republicans hated the idea initially. The US was finally starting to see real economic improvements at home, so why should they now siphon billions of dollars out overseas? Yet, before Marshall's speech took place, it had already been unanimously approved. As it turned out, the Marshall Plan was not a simple act of charity, and the Americans were looking to seize advantage of the situation. While Marshall Plan funds were to be made available to *all* European nations regardless of political affiliation (even including the communist bloc), countries that wanted money were compelled to create a unified recovery plan, which first had to be approved by the Americans. They also had to actively gear their economies toward free trade and open markets within Europe, and they had to both increase imports from and exports to the United States, granting American industries cheap supply sources and lucrative new markets for their goods. It was a clear attempt to forcibly mold European economies into the American model, and it was one of the first instances of economic imperialism in Europe, a concept that would become a theme of American power for the next five decades.

George Marshall unconvincingly tried to assure everyone in his speech that the Marshall Plan was not created to spite the USSR: "our policy is directed not against any country or doctrine [communism], but against hunger, poverty, desperation, and chaos" (Remarks by the Secretary of State at Harvard University on June 5, 1947). This simply wasn't true, and just as much as the plan was meant to entwine European economies both with the USA and each other, it was also meant to undermine the Soviets, who were not in nearly as good a position to be able to provide an alternative source of relief. With these ulterior motives, the Marshall Plan was a stunning reversal of traditional American isolationism—before the Japanese attacked Pearl Harbor, the USA had been deeply ingrained with a stubborn isolationism that insisted America and Europe remain completely separate spheres. From this point on, the US would never return to its pre-war sense of solitude and would only involve itself more and more in the affairs of the world. After such a massive investment in the European continent, the Americans have been seeking their returns ever since. Overall, the European Recovery Plan was a success, and between 1950 and 1952, most of the continent's nations had returned to their pre-war production capacity, and many had even surpassed it.

Needless to say, the Soviets hated the plan. Stalin correctly believed it was designed to undermine Soviet influence and accused them of advocating for free market capitalism, an ideology that is antithetical to Soviet communism, within nations that he believed to be within the Soviet "sphere," like Greece and Turkey. In fact, all of the money sent to Greece and Turkey under the Marshall Plan was specifically used to combat Soviet influence and to fund anti-Soviet military groups. Stalin also believed the USSR was being singled out by the plan and that it was a clear attempt by America to infiltrate Europe. Despite Stalin's paranoia, his assertions here were accurate. Somewhere around 5% of the funds allocated for the Marshall Plan were actually given to the newly created Central Intelligence Agency (CIA), the American foreign intelligence unit. The CIA used these funds to carry out various clandestine plots in Europe. They used it to spread anti-Soviet propaganda throughout Europe and bankroll groups that were actively fighting Soviet rule, as they did in Ukraine.

Still, the Marshall Plan was actually open to the Soviet Union, but Truman knew there would be no way they would accept the terms of receiving aid. Stalin flatly rejected the plan and, in fact, sought to prevent it from being accomplished. The Western nations tried several times to negotiate with the Soviets and to get them to cooperate, but Soviet Foreign Minister Vyacheslav Molotov simply walked out of the discussions after accusing his counterparts of being unduly hostile to them. At the time, the Soviets somewhat rightfully viewed themselves as the liberators of Europe, having dealt by far the most damage to the German Reich and their war machine on their march to Berlin in 1945. As they saw it, the other Allied nations were ungrateful, and this obvious attempt to challenge the Soviets in their own zone of control was unjust. In the wake of the war, the USSR had established several "satellite states" in places like Poland and Romania, countries whose governments were controlled by Stalin loyalists or outright puppets who took direct orders from Moscow. Stalin feared that if these satellite states began receiving substantial funding from anyone other than the Soviet Union, it would undermine the patriarchal nature of their relationships—if these states no longer relied on the USSR for money, they may decide to rebel and break away.

In response to the Marshall Plan, the USSR developed its own so-called Molotov Plan. It was similarly designed to provide economic relief to Soviet-influenced Eastern European nations that were coerced into rejecting the Marshall Plan. The Soviet plan was rolled out in 1947, but in reality, they had been deploying it since at least early 1945, after having developed it throughout WWII. Following the Marshall Plan's rollout, the Molotov Plan was simply renamed and intensified. The larger objectives of the Molotov Plan included garnering influence over broader portions of the continent and, eventually, morphing Europe into a massive industrial and manufacturing hub that would feed the Soviet Union's economy. The plan specifically called for the mass nationalization of industries, meaning that the state would take over and directly run them, as well as the monopolization of national resources. The satellite states would also be compelled to adopt a unified economic plan and establish trade networks to entwine their economies with the Soviet Union.

The Molotov Plan was meant to demonstrate the superiority of and inspire confidence in the Soviet communist economic system. Like the Americans, the Soviets had clear ulterior motives in pursuing these plans, but unlike the Americans, the Soviets did not have a pristine and efficient industrial economy that could fund a massive rebuilding effort. As a result, an unofficial part of the Molotov Plan involved the absolute plundering of wealth from occupied German lands to alleviate shortages in their own territories. This funneling of resources and wealth, which the Soviets considered to be reparations for the war, would fund a large portion of the Soviets' economic plans. Although some of the broader goals of the Molotov Plan were achieved, it did not have nearly as positive an impact on the war-torn European countries as the Marshall Plan did. While nations like Britain, France, and Allied-occupied Germany rose from the ashes of war to a new era of prosperity, the economies of Eastern Europe continued to flounder for years. Just two years after the war had ended, these two opposing plans had drawn a dividing line through the continent, and some consider the Marshall Plan, as well as the Soviets' rejection of it, to be the true start of the Cold War era.

Redrawing Borders

The years following 1945 saw a large number of other economic reforms and programs developed to help cure Europe. The European Economic Community, a forerunner to the modern-day European Union, served to deeply entwine European markets for the express purpose of making going to war an incredibly costly endeavor—if Germany was reliant on France for coal, for example, it would be a suicidal decision to consider making war with them again. But these years were not only characterized by economic realignment. There were also considerable political and geographic shifts that came with them. In February 1945, when victory over the Axis was already a foregone conclusion, Franklin Roosevelt, Josef Stalin, and Winston Churchill met at a conference in Yalta, a town in Crimea, to discuss post-war Europe and what the continent would look like in the coming years. The British and the Soviets were particularly at odds. Churchill wanted to see widespread, free, and democratic elections throughout Europe, and Stalin wanted clear, international acknowledgment of the Soviet sphere of influence in the lands that they had conquered. For both of these leaders, the future of Poland was a primary concern.

Between July and August 1945, another meeting was held in Potsdam, Germany, and representatives from the three nations attended again. Since Yalta, however, Clement Attlee had defeated Churchill in the British elections and replaced him at Potsdam. FDR had also died in April and was replaced by his Vice President, Harry Truman. The goal of Potsdam was to both reaffirm the agreements made at Yalta and settle on new agreements. One of the main settlements was that Poland, to the chagrin of the British, would be acknowledged as a Soviet realm and that the Provisional Government of the Republic of Poland, which was strictly communist, would be established. Stalin assured the Allies that free elections would swiftly be held to allow the Polish to determine their own destinies, but the supposed dates for these elections were continually pushed back. This deeply angered Churchill, the former Prime Minister now serving as a Member of Parliament. Rather than free elections, Poland was turned into a permanent Soviet satellite state. "Free" elections were eventually held later in 1947, but not before squads of Red Army soldiers swept through Warsaw and eliminated all those politicians deemed not loyal to Stalin. Poland, the nation whose hopes for freedom sparked WWII, has now fallen into the hands of another brutal dictator. The Western Allies had quickly become wary of the Soviets and their false promises.

Another obvious concern in these years was the future of Germany, which was also a concern addressed at Potsdam. The United States wanted to ensure that Germany, geographically close to the Soviet borders, would become a strong and democratic ally against Stalin.

With all of the German industrial power at Soviet disposal, they could pose a realistic challenge to American dominance. France, a country twice invaded by the Germans earlier in the century, was fearful of the German tradition of militarism and wanted the country totally deindustrialized. The Soviets had similar desires, wanting for a time to turn their economy into a primarily agricultural one. A powerhouse German military had led to the deaths of millions of Soviet soldiers and citizens, and they were keen to avoid this from ever happening again. Unanimity on the German question would have never been achieved, and so after Potsdam, it was agreed to split conquered Germany into four separate zones, with one zone each occupied by the USA, Britain, France, and the USSR. France controlled the smallest zone, which was made up primarily of contested lands along the French border. The American, British, and Soviet zones were roughly equal in size, but importantly, the capital of Berlin lay entirely within the Soviet zone. Berlin itself was also eventually divided into four occupation zones, a situation that, in later decades, led to the construction of the infamous Berlin Wall.

The occupation of Germany resulted in the release of all Nazi-annexed lands, with most of them reverting to their pre-war borders. All four nations that occupied Germany agreed to the process of demilitarizing the country, at least for now, in order to appease the Soviets and the French. They all also agreed to pursue "denazification," a process meant to stamp out Nazi, nationalist, and fascist ideologies from the country and to strip away the centuries-old Prussian military tradition that was prominent among German officers. This involved seeking out and arresting Nazi leaders hiding from the general public. Importantly, though, Stalin did not order the arrest of only Nazis but also wealthy landowners, capitalist business owners, and corporate leaders, all of whom were expected to be hostile to the Communist Party. The Allies also agreed to shift Germany's eastern border and push it westward to reduce the overall size of the country. Poland received all German lands east of the Neisse and Oder rivers. The process of shrinking Germany involved the forced relocation of millions of ethnic Germans out of their former homes. Several million people were displaced and left homeless, and many were unable to travel back to Germany, leaving them stateless and landless. Many of those unable to return to Germany were picked up by squads of soldiers and sent to labor camps in Soviet bloc countries.

Austria, to Germany's east, was also divided into four occupation zones and administered jointly by the Allied powers. Prior to the Second World War, Austria was completely absorbed into the German Reich in a process known as the *anschluss*, meaning "reunification," and its people were some of the most hardline Nazi supporters in Europe. The idea that led to the *anschluss* was that Austrians were Germans by blood and that Austria was an integral part of the German empire. When Nazi tanks and artillery rolled into the streets of Austria in 1938, they were met with thunderous applause and celebration by everyday Austrians, who then proceeded to go on a violent rampage against the nation's Jewish population. As a result, they suffered much the same fate as Germany did, and the terms of the *anschluss* were reversed, forever severing the two Axis nations. Across Eastern Europe, several states were organized by the USSR as satellite states whose governing parties functioned as puppets of Stalin. These included Czechoslovakia, Romania, and Hungary. In 1946, Albania and Bulgaria joined them. Yugoslavia was also essentially a Soviet puppet until they severed ties with Stalin in 1948. Within these territories, ethnic Germans were expelled, adding to the humanitarian crisis of displaced Germans on the continent.

In 1947, the US and Britain decided to merge their portions of Germany into a single entity, a move that Stalin unsurprisingly saw as anti-Soviet. Retaliation came in 1948, when Stalin chose to completely blockade the city of Berlin. The people of Berlin, a city that was still recovering from a massive bombing campaign in 1945, were struggling and in desperate need of Allied aid. The blockade prevented any aid from the US or Britain from entering Germany, and they were forced to conduct a massive operation to airlift food and other necessities into the western half of the city just to prevent mass starvation. It involved several months of nearly constant supply drops before the Soviets finally abandoned the blockade and allowed land access to the city. It was a major propaganda victory for the United States and their allies— no matter how hard the Soviets tried to stop them, they demonstrated the power and benevolence of their democratic and anti-communist way of life.

In 1949, the French occupation zone also merged with the American-British one, creating two separate Germanies, East and West. The Western nations reorganized their territory into the Federal Republic of Germany, commonly known as West Germany, a technically independent nation that was strictly allied to the United States. Months later, the Soviets responded by reorganizing their territory into the German Democratic Republic, commonly known as East Germany, the newest of the Soviet satellite states with a staunchly Stalinist government. Major issues soon arose that divided Germany further, largely as a result of the success of Western economic policies and the failures of Eastern ones. Over the years, slews of skilled East Germans, including engineers and scientists, fled across the border to West Germany. It got so bad that by the early 1950s, the Soviet and East German military aggressively patrolled the border to try to stop the bleeding. Though escapes did still happen across the East-West German border, they were largely curtailed. However, escapes from East Berlin into West Berlin were still rampant and harder to prevent. This culminated in August of 1961 when East German troops rolled out thousands of rows of barbed wire across the city's border, a physical blockade that eventually morphed into the infamous Berlin Wall.

A map of the division of East and West Germany.

As a primary aggressor in WWII, the Italians were also subject to land forfeiture in 1947. The areas of La Brigue and Tende were surrendered to France, the Dodecanese islands in the Mediterranean were given to Greece, and the new communist nation of Yugoslavia received Goriska, Istria, Zadar, and the Dalmatian islands. France, of course, was also made whole again after being partitioned by the Axis after their defeat in WWII. When they were conquered, the northern region of France was directly annexed by the Nazis, and the southern region was reorganized as an "independent" fascist state called Vichy France, or the French State. Portions of southern France were also directly seized by the Italians, which was reversed following the end of the war. Various borders across Europe were constantly fluctuating in these years; however, the overall desire was to bring Europe back to its old self, to a more familiar state. Still, territorial changes were common as the victors and victims looked to settle scores with their conquerors. The redrawing of borders post-1945 was not limited to Europe, however. European nations still had colonies all over the world in the 1940s, and the end of the war had massive consequences for the future of these lands as well, as we will soon see.

CHAPTER 3:
THE IRON CURTAIN DESCENDS

Europe has always been a land of diverse cultures, proud national identities, and independent ethnic states. In the end, the Second World War did not change this. Countries died out but were reborn from the ashes, and the conquering powers that sought to homogenize the continent were foiled. Europeans remained committed to controlling their own destinies; however, after 1945, this was a more complicated concept. Never before had the nations of Europe been under the sway of some foreign power. They were used to being the ones exerting their own power and influence. The end of WWII changed all of this. The world was becoming more black-and-white, and everyone was looking for the heroes and the villains. With only the USA and the USSR strong enough to stand on their own two feet, Europe, and indeed the world, split into two separate factions. Everyone had to pick a side, and those who didn't would be left out in the cold. The world was divided.

A Bipolar World

Several factors led to this state of affairs post-1945. During the war, European countries were in desperate need of loans, goods, and weapons. The United States was one of the few non-European countries with the industrial power to be able to service these needs, and as a result, the American economy prospered massively. Even after the US joined the war at the end of 1941, their manufacturing sector was in overdrive and was not subject to the bombing campaigns that had crippled the production capabilities of Britain and the other European Allies. When Hawaii was attacked by the Japanese, the formerly isolationist American public was roused into a sudden wartime frenzy, and people across the country were eager to participate, whether overseas or on the homefront. American factories designed to produce consumer goods were rapidly retooled and converted into wartime factories producing rifles, machine guns, ammunition, explosives, bombers, fighter planes, and naval warships. The same factories that were once producing common household electronics and children's toys were now producing tools of destruction and warfare.

The massive wartime demand for supplies created plenty of well-paying jobs for an American public that had been brutally beaten down since the depression of 1929. Labor was in high demand but scarce since so many young men were needed as soldiers overseas, resulting in high wages for those joining the workforce at home. The labor demand also resulted in millions of women joining the workforce for the first time, a development that proved to be permanent. The addition of a brand new source of labor boosted the American economy even further. When the war was over, and the soldiers returned home, many women were forced to vacate their new positions, but they had made it loud and clear that they weren't simply going to return home forever. They had become a staple of the American workforce.

Americans were moving from all over to urban centers to take jobs in the factories, and new production hubs were being built everywhere to support and supply both the American and European militaries. The need for wartime goods was so strong that the manufacture of some civilian goods virtually stopped completely. Before America joined the war, US automakers were producing millions of automobiles per year. From 1942 to 1945, however, they produced less than 150. The entire automotive industry pivoted to the war effort, and companies like Ford Motors ceased building streetcars in favor of fighter planes and bombers. The recovery of America after 1941 was nothing short of miraculous, and in combination with President Roosevelt's economic policies, the Great Depression in America was quickly fading completely. During the peak of the Great Depression, the USA achieved an unemployment rate of nearly 25%. After the industrial boom of the 1940s, this had dropped to almost 1%, the lowest unemployment in American history (Vergun, 2020). With Pearl Harbor being the only successful attack on American soil for the duration of the war, these burgeoning industries were also safe from the hells that the factories of London, Birmingham, and Bristol were subjected to. The Second World War had transformed the American economy into a powerhouse of manufacturing.

On the part of the Soviet Union, their rise to global power was less predictable than that of America's, and they certainly had a less auspicious start to the 1940s. Prior to the outbreak of WWII, a series of embarrassing military blunders had led most of the rest of the world to see the Soviet Union as weak, backward, and technologically outdated. Particularly after the massive Soviet Red Army utterly failed to conquer the small nation of Finland in 1939, the communists were seen as incapable of posing a serious threat. Hitler and Nazi Germany became confident that the USSR would completely collapse the moment the *Wehrmacht* crossed the border into Soviet territory. Britain, France, and the United States were of similar minds and believed that there was no way the Soviets could withstand more than a few months of German assault. Yet, to the shock of the world, it was the Soviets that first turned the tide of the war and dealt the most severe damage to the Axis powers.

While the other Allied nations idled and waited for their opportunity, it was the Soviet Red Army that almost single-handedly held the German war machine at bay. It was the Red Army that the world saw marching through the streets of newly-occupied Berlin, and it was Soviet soldiers that cut down the Nazi flag over the German Reichstag building and replaced it with the hammer and sickle banner. Meanwhile, Britain, the nation with the strongest overseas empire and the most powerful navy on the planet, was nearly bombed out of existence. France, the nation widely regarded as possessing the most disciplined and effective land army on the continent prior to 1939, was utterly dominated in a matter of weeks. The USSR had proved its mettle and demonstrated what the Soviet people were capable of when focused on a common goal. The almost pathological sense of national pride and faith in communism had awoken in the Soviet Union, and by the time their industry had been geared toward wartime production, they found themselves in a position to easily push across the continent if they wanted to. The prospect of Soviet domination became a terrifying thought in the minds of Europeans, Asians, and Americans.

Still, the Soviets did not make it out of the war unscathed, as the Americans did. Soviet industry had already taken years to catch up to its European contemporaries, plus it had been severely damaged by German attacks. They still had significant production capabilities, but they could not match America's. Instead, Soviet power came from the fact that as the Red Army was marching across Europe en route to destroy the German Reich, they installed friendly and cooperative communist governments along the way. The lands they crossed during the war were never really given up after peace, and this was true in the East and the West. When the USSR began invading Japanese territory near the end of the war, they pushed southward across the Korean peninsula toward the sea. When Japan surrendered, the place where the Red Army stopped marching became the new border between North and South Korea. The South was occupied by the Western Allies and was pro-democratic and pro-American. The North became another Soviet puppet state. In 1948, they installed dictator Kim Il Sung, the leader of a political dynasty that has ruled North Korea ever since.

So, at the conclusion of the war, the Soviet Union was still in a tough economic position, but they were at the center of a massive sphere of influence and commanded the loyalty of a large grouping of Eastern European and Asian territory. Their land army was also massive, owing to the large population living within the vast Soviet territory. Despite their millions of deaths, there were so many able-bodied young men to throw into the meat grinder that there were realistic fears that, if they desired to, they could pose an even graver threat to the Western Allies once Germany was defeated. They could have easily sparked yet another global war immediately after the conclusion of World War II. The Allies, particularly Churchill and Truman, saw the Soviets as such a dire threat that drastic measures and powerful shows of force were necessary. The Second World War needed to end with a literal bang, and that bang was to take place at the expense of the Japanese population.

Although the Americans and Soviets had become close allies in the fight against Hitler and Nazism, the two nations were deeply and irreparably divided along ideological lines. Most of the West genuinely feared Soviet-style communism and viewed it as antithetical to Western civilization, free market capitalism, and Judeo-Christian religious values. The Soviets, in turn, viewed capitalist nations as imperialist, oppressive, and an affront to basic humanity. They believed their economic systems were inherently exploitative, and they made it their national mission to encourage and forcibly install communist regimes across the world. Soviet influence was far-reaching and felt deeply even in America's own backyard, which had dramatic and terrifying consequences in the coming decades.

As early as 1946, the diverging path that the world was on was already clear to world leaders. That year, Winston Churchill spoke at an event in Fulton, Missouri, where he outlined his vision for the coming future:

A shadow has fallen upon the scenes so lately lighted by the Allied victory. Nobody knows what Soviet Russia and its communist international organization intends to do in the immediate future, or what are the limits, if any, to their expansive and proselytizing tendencies. I have a strong admiration and regard for the valiant Russian people and for my wartime comrade, Marshal Stalin. . .it is my duty, however, to place before you certain facts about the present position in Europe. From Stettin in the Baltic to Trieste in the Adriatic, an iron curtain has descended across the continent. Behind that line lie all the capitals of the ancient states of Central and Eastern Europe. Warsaw, Berlin, Prague, Vienna, Budapest, Belgrade, Bucharest, and Sofia, all these famous cities and the populations around them lie in the Soviet sphere and all are subject in one form or another, not only to Soviet influence but to a very high and increasing measure of control from Moscow. . .this is certainly not the liberated Europe we fought to build up. Nor is it one which contains the essentials of permanent peace, (National Archives, 1946).

Churchill, as it turned out, was very accurate. This "iron curtain," a term coined by Churchill, was a hint at the developing state of Europe, and it was a term that defined much of the political climate from 1946 until the 1990s.

Dawn of the Atomic Age

After Churchill's speech, tensions were even higher across the developed world. The thought of another conflict breaking out, one with an even wider scope than WWII, was immeasurably more dangerous, given the fact that the Americans had proven their willingness to use atomic weapons against their enemies, including civilians. The very existence of this destructive technology made any conflict more serious, and everyone knew it was only a matter of time before the knowledge of how to replicate these weapons spread throughout the world, including to the rapidly developing Soviet Union. Even many American leaders were not thrilled with the idea of introducing atomic weapons to the world. Top military brass like Admirals William Leahy and William Halsey, and even Supreme Commander and future US President Dwight D. Eisenhower, were deeply opposed to their use. Many more had serious moral reservations about using them in civilian areas. President Truman's determination didn't waver, though, and the prospect of Stalin continuing his conquest of Japanese land was unacceptable. If the Japanese home islands were, in the worst-case scenario, transformed into a Soviet puppet state, there would be no hope of combating the spread of communism in Asia through the 1940s and 1950s. Giving Stalin a preview of a weapon that could level Moscow was, apparently, the only reasonable option.

The hope was that if the world could see what the unleashing of atomic energy, a power only the Americans had yet mastered, was capable of, peace after the war would be assured. Other nations with a mind to continue the war would certainly be kept in line. In a way, the bombings of Hiroshima and Nagasaki were precursor events to the United States taking up the role of "world police," a power capable of meting out punishment and discipline to nations that act inappropriately. This new role would serve to secure American interests for decades. Most importantly, Hiroshima and Nagasaki signaled the beginning of what came to be known as the Atomic Age, a period of time marked by the use and fear of nuclear technology. With the explosive power that these weapons could produce, combined with the toxic and poisonous levels of radiation they unleashed, it had become immediately clear in 1945 that if another World War broke out and atomic weapons were used to fight it, it could very well mean the end of civilization as we know it. Quite literally, military leaders around the world had begun thinking to themselves, "Have we finally gone too far?"

Little Boy and Fat Man, the products of the minds of the greatest scientists and engineers on earth, were a world apart from anything yet seen. The fact that more and more of these weapons were being produced daily, even as the peace of WWII was being signed, was a legitimate source of anxiety for Americans and Europeans alike. This anxiety persisted through the years as more advanced and powerful versions of these weapons were developed and tested for use. However, this technological advancement was not one-sided; after the Japanese bombings, the Soviet Union realized immediately that they, too, needed to develop their own atomic weapons if they wanted any hope of remaining a global superpower and being able to challenge the authority of the United States. American military leaders were well aware that the Soviets were going to begin creating their own arsenal of nuclear weapons as soon as they could and estimated that by about 1952–1953, Soviet scientists would have cracked the secret and unlocked the power of weaponized atomic energy. Once again, though, the Soviets had been severely underestimated. In August of 1949, at a testing site in Soviet Kazakhstan, to the shock of the Americans, Stalin's military conducted a successful test of their first nuclear bomb, "First Lightning," a full three years ahead of schedule. The power differential had been equalized.

President Truman and his generals now knew that they had officially missed their opportunity to strike at the Soviets without fear of retaliation. Now, a nuclear attack against the USSR virtually guaranteed a nuclear response against the European nations of Britain, France, West Germany, and others. This kicked off the era of nuclear proliferation and a decades-long nuclear arms race between the Western bloc, led by the USA, and the Eastern bloc, led by the Soviet Union. Each side scrambled to create the newest, biggest, and most powerful bomb to strike fear into their enemies. With each new advancement, the world was brought one step closer to the edge of suicide. Atomic energy, however, was not limited to terrifying military uses. The period from 1945–1949 was also marked by the rise of nuclear fission power plants, which used energy from radioactive materials like enriched uranium to power entire cities. These plants had no need to burn toxic coal and release their pollution into the atmosphere, and in fact, they produced hardly any waste at all. It was a safer and more efficient way to produce energy for a growing population. That is, of course, until something goes wrong. Indeed, the idea of harnessing the power of the atom was a new, fascinating, and terrifying concept that promised both wonderful benefits—clean, renewable energy—and terrible futures—nuclear annihilation.

Both the USA and USSR understood that the coming decades would be determined, more than anything else, by technological advancement. This was clear even before WWII ended but became imperative after the introduction of atom bombs. So, after the surrender of the Axis powers, both nations raced to plunder the resources of Nazi Germany, and one of their most valuable resources by far was scientific knowledge. During the war, Nazi scientists worked on and experimented with tech and scientific concepts that other nations often never even considered, including researching so-called "wonder weapons" that could ensure German victory. While many of these experiments went nowhere, they did make some stunning breakthroughs in a variety of fields, particularly rocket technology, which was still in its infancy. Their knowledge of cutting-edge scientific concepts was considered vital, and the Americans and Soviets sought to recruit these scientists for their own weapons and space programs. For the Soviet Union's part, their strategy was simply to force Nazi scientists to come with them to

Moscow under threat of death or the deaths of their families, where they would essentially be used as slave labor to create new rockets, missiles, and other weapons. The Americans offered something better, however. They offered these men, who otherwise may have been tried as war criminals, their very own slice of the American Dream. They offered a chance at a new life across the ocean, an opportunity to start again with their families as American citizens, with all the benefits that entailed. With their only options being poverty in Germany, slavery in the USSR, or a war crime tribunal, many of these Nazis unsurprisingly desired to go with the Americans.

Obviously, the recruitment of some of the worst criminals in the Reich would be a difficult pill to swallow for the American public. They couldn't simply bring them to the country and merge them into American society without an uproar—after all, this was the same nation that was adamant that these men be brought to justice for their crimes. So, a more delicate and secretive approach was required. In a clandestine operation that came to be known as Operation Paperclip, special agents of the American Counter-Intelligence Corps (CIC) recruited over 1,500 Nazi scientists between 1945 and 1959 and secretly brought them to America, along with their families. It was designed to secure their minds for America as much as it was designed to keep them away from the Soviet Union. Some of those in the government who were privy to the plan were deeply opposed to the idea of offering war criminals and Nazis a safe haven in their own backyards, and Truman did order the intelligence services specifically to avoid those deemed to be "active" Nazi supporters and those thought to be genuine war criminals. This order was, however, almost entirely ignored by those carrying out Paperclip. The recruiting agents were known to often destroy any evidence of war crimes committed by those they were trying to shuttle out of Germany. In their minds, if the United States was too selective and rejected certain scientists, they would inevitably fall into the hands of the Soviets, who would not care one way or another what crimes they had committed.

The knowledge that these men held was a boon to the American and Soviet scientific communities, and they helped to rapidly advance their respective weapons and space exploration projects. Their expertise in rocketry was critical both in helping the Soviets become the first nation to travel into space and in helping the Americans be the first nation to send men to the moon. They were also fundamental in developing the world's first rocket-propelled nuclear weapons. One of these men was Wernher von Braun, a Nazi Party member, schutzstaffel (SS) member, and the mastermind behind the German V2 rockets, which were used to devastate the cities of Britain, France, Luxembourg, and Belgium during the final years of the war. Von Braun was one of the many top Nazi scientists that were brought to the US via Operation Paperclip and enlisted in the National Aeronautics and Space Administration (NASA) when it was founded in 1958. Von Braun himself became a high-ranking member of NASA and was key in America's early space exploration. Before this, though, his focus was on advancing America's capability to hit the Soviet Union with nuclear missiles. He spearheaded the development of the PGM-11 Redstone, the first American nuclear-equipped ballistic missile. He also worked on theoretical plans to create an American space station armed with military personnel with the ability to strike anywhere on Earth with nuclear weapons.

With this German technical knowledge in their inventory, the USA and USSR engaged in a high-speed race to craft weapons that would categorically outclass the enemy. In the years following Paperclip, the nuclear arms race progressed to such a stage that the two nations operated under the mentality of MAD, or Mutual Assured Destruction. This was the idea that if both nations possessed vast stockpiles of powerful atomic bombs, peace would be more, not less, assured. Since a nuclear attack on one nation would inevitably provoke a rapid nuclear response, both sides would be too hesitant to ever actually launch their weapons since it would almost certainly mean the utter annihilation of their own country. Also known as "brinksmanship," the state of constantly being on the edge of war, it was paradoxically assured that war would never break out. The limits of this idea were put to the test when the nuclear arms race culminated in 1962 with a showdown between the USA and the USSR that very nearly resulted in nuclear war. Even after this historic moment, fear of the atom and its power lingered for decades. War was no longer war, and there were no longer just "bombs." Now, there was *the* bomb.

CHAPTER 4:
THE COLD WAR

The "iron curtain" that Winston Churchill envisioned descending over Europe in 1946 was not physical in any way, but it was certainly deeply felt. The European air itself was tense and thick with anxiety. The political fissure that seemed to widen with each passing day was already having severe impacts and immediate repercussions both on the homefront and on international relationships. Global politics were morphing into something potentially even scarier than what the world witnessed in the 1930s, something that threatened not just the conquest of Europe but the destruction of the entire world. It seemed that on either side of the Iron Curtain, completely separate worlds existed in their own self-contained hemispheres. New fears of the "other" were born, and new alliances were formed. The questions remained: how far was the United States willing to go to defeat their new juggernaut of an enemy, and how far was the USSR willing to go to promote their communist ideology throughout the world? These questions and the fear they induced defined the era known as the Cold War.

Espionage and the Red Scare

Fear of Soviet communism was, of course, not limited to continental Europe. The United States, once a wartime ally of Stalin, descended into a black chasm of fear and alarmism that was even worse than the situation in Western Europe. The relationship between the two nations had so suddenly turned into a bitter rivalry that suspicions and paranoia over communist infiltration ran wild, becoming a major daily concern on the American homefront. The period following 1946 was not, however, the first time the American public fell prey to anxiety over the spread of communism. At its basest level, communism is an ideology that calls for a future in which laborers come to control the means of goods production (i.e., factories, farmlands, and their equipment), ousting the corporate class of rich owners and instituting a government run by the working class, before ultimately dissolving government altogether. It was essentially an economic doctrine, and it was largely theoretical until 1917 when the first officially communist state came into being—the USSR. Across the sea in America, a nation whose economy and government rested on the free market and corporate foundations, politicians became stressed over the idea that this toxic ideology could spread and take root in their own homes. This fear trickled downward, and the American people were roused into a panic. Americans turned on Americans. Those guilty of nothing more than advocating for workers' rights were fired, ostracized, and blacklisted. The First Red Scare gripped America from 1917 until the early 1920s (the color red became associated with communism, and communists became known as "Reds," a reference to the color of the Soviet flag).

With the fall of the Iron Curtain, the Red Scare in America returned with renewed vigor. During this time, both the USA and USSR engaged in espionage and employed secret agents and spies that were meant to infiltrate and report on their enemy's government. In 1945, though, most Americans were still reveling in the victory of WWII and too excited over the return of their young men to worry about the new enemy on the horizon. Later that year, however, an American woman named Elizabeth Bentley, who had been feeding American government information to the Soviets since the mid-1930s, decided to defect. After falling out with her superiors based in Moscow, Bentley willingly approached the FBI and surrendered a list of several American government officials and employees of the Office of Strategic Services who she described as spies working for the NKVD (the Soviet interior ministry, which functioned as a secret police and spy unit). When this news broke, there was a rejuvenated hysteria in the American public, and society at large became fearful of a communist takeover.

The government moved quickly. In order to combat the supposedly deep communist influence in Congress and the Senate, the House of Representatives' Un-American Activities Committee (HUAC), which had been used sporadically since 1917, became a permanent congressional committee. Their mandate was clear: Root out any and all behavior that was deemed "un-American." This invariably referred to communism. HUAC began staging aggressive, probing investigations and interrogations of government employees who were suspected of having any communist sympathies. In 1948, Alger Hiss, a high-ranking government official in Truman's administration, was accused of being a communist by HUAC and another former communist, Whittaker Chambers. In a dramatic exchange over several HUAC hearings, Hiss was eventually sent to prison, which did nothing to assuage the nation's anxiety. Communists, it appeared, were everywhere. The federal HUAC terrorized those public figures unlucky enough to be accused, but many states also had their own local "mini" HUACs organized by the state legislatures. Most of these didn't last longer than a few years, except in California, where "inquisitors stalked the state for an extraordinary three decades" (Heale, 1998). Incredibly, some states even called for the execution of those determined to be communists, but this proved too extreme for the American people to accept.

In March of 1947, before the Hiss scandal, President Truman created the Federal Employees Loyalty Program. The organizers of the program were responsible for conducting large-scale investigations of federal employees at all levels of the government. They staged invasive interrogations that were designed to discern the political loyalties of government officials and to determine their level of "Americanism." Truman went all-in on the persecution in order to protect himself from accusations of being too lenient on communists. Truman was the Vice President of FDR, the man behind the groundbreaking New Deal economic policies that helped reverse the Great Depression. Many Americans, particularly Republicans, viewed the New Deal as blatantly communist legislation and believed that Truman was inextricably tied to it. To prove his capitalist credentials, Truman demanded that federal employees take loyalty oaths, whereby employees had to swear allegiance to the American way of life and the system of government as outlined in the Constitution. This necessarily meant the denunciation of communist forms of government. Between the program's start in 1947 and 1956, over 2,500 government employees were fired, and

12,000 resigned from their posts as a direct result of the witch hunt (Kirkendall, 2013).

All this led to an era of mistrust in the American government. Based on the belief that communism was inherently subversive, American politicians believed that exposure was the best tool to fight it. So, there was a concerted effort to ensure that Americans at large were actively afraid of and alert to the possibility of infiltration. It was thought that even if not all the people accused were actually communists, hauling them before Congress and interrogating them would nevertheless be beneficial to the goal of shining as much light as possible on potential spies. If everyone, even slightly left-wing, was being accused, the idea of agreeing to spy for the Soviets would be far less enticing. As long-time FBI Director J. Edgar Hoover said himself to HUAC in 1947, "victory will be assured once communists are identified and exposed" (quoted in Heale, 1998). Hoover remained one of the staunchest anti-communists in America and used his power as head of the FBI to spy on those believed to be sympathetic to the "reds."

Generally, right-wing Republicans were the most vehement opponents of communism and the most fearful of it. Even with all Truman did to destroy the right to privacy of government employees, they still accused him of being soft on reds and pulling America closer to Soviet-style economics. In reality, though, the Republican Party often used Red Scare tactics against the Democratic Party as a way to reverse their party's long-suffering political fortunes. After more than 15 straight years of Democratic Presidencies, Republicans were desperately clinging to relevancy and any hope of ever winning the Presidency again. FDR had been incredibly popular, winning four consecutive elections beginning in 1933, and Truman, his successor, finished FDR's fourth term before winning an election of his own. The Red Scare presented an ideal opportunity for Republicans to regain their popularity by smearing the progressivism of the Democrats as communist-adjacent. Still, there were many Democrats who got caught up in the anti-communist fervor and turned against their colleagues and even their own constituents. In fact, almost all forms of political dissent after 1945 were interpreted as communist plotting. Leaders of the labor and union movements were some of the prime targets, as well as prominent Civil Rights leaders. Even Martin Luther King Jr. faced accusations of being a Soviet sympathizer intent on subverting American democracy.

Various American sectors and industries came under fire, but few more so than the Hollywood film industry elite. Actors, directors, and especially screenwriters, received intense scrutiny. In 1952, famed director Elia Kazan, under some duress, willingly named several of his closest friends and colleagues as communist subversives and identified them with HUAC. This permanently tarnished Kazan's reputation and goodwill in the film industry, and it provoked even more investigation into Hollywood. A few years later, in 1956, largely as a result of Elia Kazan's blabbing, Marilyn Monroe's husband, playwright Arthur Miller, was brought in to testify before HUAC regarding his political loyalties. Even Monroe herself came under suspicion by the FBI simply for being associated with Miller, and it was so concerning that her friends and colleagues advised her to divorce Miller or risk her career imploding. The Kazan debacle was not nearly the first of Hollywood's Red Scare woes, however.

In 1947, several prominent filmmakers, famously known as the "Hollywood Ten," were ordered to testify before HUAC, which they refused to do out of principle. As a result, studio executives issued a "blacklist," a collection of names of individuals who the industry leaders agreed should not be employed by *any* studio. Government pressure was strong, and no studio wanted to risk the ire of the vehemently anti-communist Truman administration, so they were eager to ban anyone they suspected of being a target of HUAC. Many big studios even began producing anti-communist films at the behest of the government, including the hilariously named *I Married a Communist* (1949), produced by the prestigious RKO Pictures. Once responsible for producing some of the most beloved films of all time, including *King Kong* and *Citizen Kane*, RKO had been reduced to peddling propaganda pieces. Also in 1949, Republic Pictures released *The Red Menace*, in which an American WWII veteran is seduced into joining the American Communist Party and only comes to his senses when he witnesses a fellow member being executed for questioning Party officials. In 1952, United Artists' *Red Planet Mars* hit theaters, a science fiction film that heavily implied that the world's constant fear of nuclear annihilation may be a kind of divine punishment for humanity's attraction to "godless" communism. By the conclusion of the film, the Soviet Union has been happily overthrown and replaced by a Christian theocracy.

The Red Scare was also a time when career opportunists tried to forge names for themselves. Smearing the reputations of your colleagues was apparently a convenient way to promote your own, as Joseph McCarthy, a relatively unknown Senator from Wisconsin, discovered in 1950. Early that year, McCarthy delivered a lengthy speech to the Republican Women's Club in the town of Wheeling, West Virginia, where he claimed that he was personally aware of dozens of members of the State Department who were, in fact, covert communists. The speech made national news and agitated the public, and McCarthy suddenly became a household name that commanded attention. It did quickly become clear, however, that McCarthy was exaggerating, if not outright lying. He continued to make speeches claiming knowledge of secret subversives, but each time, he provided a different, more fantastic number. In Salt Lake City, just days after Wheeling, he claimed there were nearly 60. When he later spoke before the Senate in a tiring 5-hour tirade, the number was inflated to over 80.

McCarthy had established himself as a crusader, one who would rest at nothing to root out the supposed communist influence seeping into American life as a result of Soviet interference. He also proved that he was not above spreading rumors and hearsay about his colleagues or using intimidation and fear-mongering to scare the public into supporting his ventures. In the process of building a name for himself, McCarthy quickly became one of the most feared politicians in the country, and upsetting him meant risking being accused of having communist sympathies. He cost countless people their careers, including politicians, Hollywood elites, and many left-wing university academics and administrators. His tactics were undoubtedly aggressive, but at the time, he had credibility. Many American fears of infiltration were once again vindicated in 1950, when Julius and Ethel Rosenberg were arrested for suspicion of espionage. The married couple had initially met as members of the Young Communist League in New York, of which Julius was a leading figure. Since about 1942, the pair have been engaged in covert spying, and Julius has been supplying information and protected documents to the NKVD in Moscow. During the war, Julius was working for the Army Signal Corps in Fort Monmouth, where research was being carried out on innovations in radar and missile technology, both of which Julius was eager to share with the USSR. Their crowning achievement, however, was the recruitment of several other spies, including Russell McNutt and David Greenglass, who both worked on the top-secret Manhattan Project, the initiative that developed the Little Boy and Fat Man nuclear weapons. The secrets this spy ring funneled overseas helped to massively accelerate the Soviet nuclear program.

When the role the Rosenbergs played came to light, they were meant to be made an example of. There wasn't plenty of concrete proof at the time, but there was enough for the ravenous American government and the public. The Rosenbergs were unsurprisingly convicted of espionage on behalf of a foreign enemy, and they received the maximum penalty. In 1953, in the infamous Sing Sing prison, Julius and Ethel were executed via electric shock. Their accusation, conviction, and execution provided plenty of fuel for the fire that McCarthy had been stoking for 3 years, and many who were previously critical of the witch hunts were forced to consider that maybe McCarthy was right all along. In 1953, he received his own committee in the Senate, which he used as a tool to stage even more aggressive interrogations. Eventually, though, McCarthy went too far, and his fellow Senators believed he had become too powerful and tyrannical. In 1954, he was censured and denounced by his Senate colleagues, bringing the era of "McCarthyist" paranoia and fear to an end, though the general fear of communism was still strong.

McCarthy was put on the back burner by the mid-1950s, but the same year he was censured, the government officially banned the American Communist Party by passing the Communist Control Act of

1954. Members of the Party had been actively persecuted since at least 1948, but this Act forced its very existence into the black market of ideas. Developments around the world continued to convince Americans that communism was a vile, invasive way of life. The outbreak of the Korean War and the establishment of the communist, Soviet-aligned People's Republic of China in 1951 caused many to fear that the entire Eastern half of the world was doomed to fall to communism. It also led to intense suspicion and distrust toward Asian Americans, many of whom were already marginalized due to Japan's role in WWII. Now, the Chinese (or anyone who looked vaguely Chinese) were a compromised people. Who knew where their real loyalties lied? To combat these perceived threats, the Senate Internal Security Subcommittee, or SISS, was created in 1951 under Truman's administration, which focused both on internal affairs and foreign policy in regards to Asia. After the Republicans regained the White House with the 1952 election of WWII hero Dwight D. Eisenhower, the SISS was taken over by mostly right-wingers, and they took an even more aggressive stance toward the Asian communists. As we can see, this will have many important knock-on effects on the United States in the coming years.

The era of the Red Scare was certainly not limited to the US. In America's neighboring Canada, there was also a miniature Red Scare, which was propelled to national attention in 1947. That year, a Member of Parliament from the province of Quebec named Fred Rose was found guilty of spying for the Soviets after Igor Gouzenko, an employee at the Soviet embassy in Ottawa, was recalled to his homeland by Moscow. Rather than return to the USSR, Gouzenko opted to defect and remain in Canada. As a peace offering to his new home, Gouzenko exposed to Canadian authorities a massive spy ring operating in both Canada and the United States, of which Rose was a main leader. The scandal shook Canadian and American policymakers, and Rose was later imprisoned and deported to his native Poland. Fred Rose remains the only member of the Canadian Communist Party to ever hold a seat in parliament and the only one to be convicted of espionage for a foreign power. In the USSR, too, there was a kind of reverse Red Scare, during which the Soviet government was in constant fear of dissent. Particularly during the reign of Stalin, the elder statesmen of the USSR were on the hunt for anyone who may not have been fully convinced of the superiority of the Soviet system as dictated by Stalin. In this period, the Soviet government was known for its purges, in which large numbers of government officials were executed, imprisoned, or deposed for their perceived slights against the Communist Party. Elsewhere around the world, nations and communities turned in on themselves as a result of the new bipolar dynamic, pitting the capitalist West against the communist East. Still, no other country even approached the United States when it came to what they were willing to do to win. Beginning with President Truman and his geopolitical theories, the United States was focusing not just on anti-communism at home but on a massive, global scale.

The Domino Theory and Truman's Doctrine of Containment

The so-called "domino theory" was a geopolitical concept that flourished in the years after WWII. Basically, the theory suggested social and political shifts in one region would typically spill over and affect other neighboring regions, thus causing a chain reaction of "falling dominoes." The theory was around for a long time before WWII, but the insidious spread of fascism through Europe proved to have nearly apocalyptic consequences. Beginning in Italy, fascist ideology traveled north to Germany and Austria and west to Spain. Nazi sympathizers in France, Britain, America, and elsewhere attempted to establish their own fascist political movements to the alarm of lovers of democracy everywhere. Allowing these "dominos" to continue to fall nearly led to the end of freedom in Europe, and the world was keen to avoid the mistakes of the past. In the mid-1940s and 1950s, the US leaned into the domino theory much more heavily, believing that the threat of communist spread was even more insidious, subversive, and anti-democratic than that posed by the Nazis and fascists. Proponents of the domino theory believed that as countries around the world turned communist, the poisonous ideology would spread indefinitely. This had to be avoided at all costs, and even one domino falling was too much to accept.

In one sense, American belief in the domino theory was a little ironic. American leaders simultaneously claimed that communism was an awful, authoritarian system in which everyone loses while also claiming that it was such an attractive ideology to the people that it would sweep across entire continents if there was no intervention. This irony was apparently lost on Truman's administration. Inspired by the implications of the domino theory, Truman and his ministers developed what came to be known as the Truman Doctrine of Containment. The doctrine became a critical aspect of US foreign policy for years, and it asserted that the global rise of "authoritarianism" had to be contained wherever it may pop up. Despite the wording, in the Cold War context, "authoritarian" almost exclusively meant communist, and its real goal was simply to prevent global governments from adopting Soviet-style systems. The doctrine pledged American economic and potentially military support to any nations struggling from external or internal "authoritarian" threats, which was unsurprisingly used as a pretext for the United States to meddle in the affairs of sovereign countries. Still, Truman always marketed the idea as a benevolent mission to free the world of tyranny:

> "One of the primary objectives of the foreign policy of the United States is the creation of conditions in which we and other nations will be able to work out a way of life free from coercion. This was a fundamental issue in the war with Germany and Japan. Our victory was won over countries which sought to impose their will, and their way of life, upon other nations," (address of President Truman in Congress, March 12, 1947).

In reality, there was truth to the domino theory that convinced many Americans that the Truman Doctrine was both justified and admirable. One common theme among newly-established communist states throughout the 20th century was that they almost always went on to fund the communist parties in their neighboring countries. This was the case both with the USSR in Eastern Europe and, after 1949, China in Eastern Asia. The Chinese communists supported the communist movements in Indochina and Korea, and China was, in turn, supported by the USSR. Even small communist states like Yugoslavia and Bulgaria helped support the efforts of both Greek and Turkish communists. Support was especially strong during times of conflict. Whenever communist states were fighting either domestic or foreign enemies, there was an almost constant exchange of aid between them. This display of solidarity led the Americans to respond in kind, pouring money and resources into nations they believed were potential targets of communist takeover. In the early years after the war, two of the most important cases of the Truman Doctrine in effect were Greece and Turkey, in Europe's Far East.

For some time, the Soviets had been exerting pressure on both Greece and Turkey to surrender access to the Black Sea and the Straits into the Mediterranean to the USSR, and Stalin had made direct threats to Turkey to try to seize full control over the sea routes. Both countries had been receiving support from Britain for some time in order to bolster their efforts against the Soviets, but in February of 1947, the British informed the Americans that funding the two nations while Britain itself was still recovering was becoming too expensive. By April, the British planned to cease all support for the anticommunists in the country, and Truman quickly realized that the burden was to fall on him and his taxpayers. In his impassioned 1947 speech before Congress, Truman explicitly referred to the domino theory when garnering support for sending aid to Greece and Turkey. If either of the two countries were allowed to fall to Soviet pressure, then the other would surely follow soon after. If they both fell, what would be next for the region? Would Italy turn communist? Iran? Or worse, the oil-rich Arab Gulf? It was a situation that demanded urgency, and Truman skillfully rallied support:

> I believe we must assist free peoples to work out their own destinies in their own ways… should we fail to aid Greece and Turkey in this fateful hour, the effect will be far-reaching to the West as well as to the East. We must take immediate and resolute action," (quoted in Satterthwaite, 1972).

The American plan was already approved, and the US ended up sending a massive amount of aid to both countries. Turkey, in particular, received an immense amount of funding to rebuild its troubled economy. American leaders still firmly believed that economic struggles and uncertainty were key factors in communist takeovers, so their investment in Turkey was directly influenced by the Containment Doctrine. The effects, both in the short and long term, were incredible, and the economic recovery in Turkey was nothing short of a miracle—at the same time, communist elements in the country were suppressed. A key justification for Truman's doctrine was opposition to the meddling of foreign powers in the affairs of smaller nations, but it should be clear by now that this was a blatant irony. The Soviets did indeed seek to subvert independent governments, but Truman, in addition to several subsequent administrations, actively encroached upon the freedom of other countries and sought to control internal affairs all across the world.

NATO and the Warsaw Pact

In 1949, the Hungarian People's Republic, an obvious Soviet puppet government, was established. The year prior, the Soviets successfully supported a coup in Czechoslovakia, which produced yet another Soviet-aligned state. These events, among others, worried the West. To deter further expansion into Western Europe, talks began to establish the mutual defense of American-aligned nations. In 1949, as a direct challenge to Soviet hegemony, the United States, Canada, and their European allies banded together in a military alliance. Final discussions concluded in April 1949, and the result was the formal creation of the North Atlantic Treaty Organization (NATO). At first, there were 12 original signatories: America, Britain, Canada, France, Italy, Luxembourg, Belgium, Portugal, Denmark, the Netherlands, Norway, and even far-away Iceland. Spain, still under the fascistic dictatorship of Francisco Franco, was not included. Over the coming years, several more nations joined NATO, looking for the American protection that NATO guaranteed. As per the guidelines of the Treaty, if just one of these nations were targeted for an invasion or attack by "foreign powers," i.e., the communists, it would be treated as an assault against the entire alliance, thus pulling in the military weight of a large portion of Europe. In the event of all-out nuclear warfare, it would be clear where the battle lines would be.

Of course, the Americans were not alone in forming these kinds of international pacts. In 1947, the Soviets created the Cominform, which basically functioned like a massive information bureau composed of the world's communist parties. Member nations could freely collect and exchange relevant information on geopolitics, ensuring they were keeping up with the West. Two years later, Comecon was formed, which was an organization designed to coordinate and standardize the economic development of communist countries, including the USSR, Hungary, Poland, and Czechoslovakia. In just a short period of time following WWII, nearly every single European nation came to be affiliated, officially or otherwise, with the American or Soviet bloc. Those who believed the death of Adolf Hitler and Nazi ideology was to be the dawn of a new era of peace in Europe now felt as though they were standing on the edge of the abyss, dreading the future that they foresaw.

Both powers were organizing, but by 1950, the Soviet bloc still did not have an official military defense treaty that could challenge the might of NATO. That is, until the mid-1950s, when the Soviet Union and their satellites created the Treaty of Friendship, Cooperation, and Mutual Assistance, also known as the Warsaw Pact. There were originally seven signatories plus the USSR, including Albania, Romania, Hungary,

Bulgaria, Poland, Czechoslovakia, and the 6-year-old nation of East Germany. The Pact was created in response to the formation of NATO, but the main driving factor was Germany's problem. In May of 1955, the American-aligned West Germany was inducted into NATO, which many believed was the first step in the West's plan to turn Germany into a weapon against the Soviets. Since the birth of the Soviet nation in 1917, they feared a unified, militarized Germany, believing that their Prussian military traditions and ideals made Germans an inherently warlike people. The fact that West Germany was now being allowed to host a standing army and that they were in direct opposition to the Soviet bloc was something Stalin couldn't abide by. It took barely one week after West Germany's induction into NATO for the communists to announce the creation of the Warsaw Pact. The alliance system that was now being created from California in the West all the way to Serbia in the East was reminiscent of the web of treaties that dragged the planet into the First World War, and this foreboding was not lost on anyone. The entire world was walking on eggshells.

The Warsaw Pact was indeed meant as a mutual defense agreement, but in reality, the most important aspect of it was the internal security measures that it established. These allowed for much tighter military controls over the population in Soviet-aligned member states and allowed the militaries to legally step in and brutally put down revolts against the communist parties in the other countries. The Hungarian Uprising of 1956 is a case in point: the nationwide rebellion against the Hungarian puppets in government led to immediate military action as Soviet tanks and soldiers rumbled into the country and slaughtered thousands of protesters. Outside of the Warsaw Pact, important communist alliances had already formed elsewhere, particularly in

Asia, much of which the USSR also considered its sphere of influence. After the 1949 victory of the Chinese communists, Stalin and Chinese leader Mao Tse-Tung signed the Sino-Soviet Treaty of Friendship, Alliance, and Mutual Assistance, which established a political and economic alliance between two massive communist powers with a combined population that dwarfed that of the United States. The agreement ensured Chinese allegiance to Marxist-Leninist principles (named for Communist pioneers Karl Marx and Vladimir Lenin) for years. The world had indeed been splitting apart ever since 1945, but the years between the formation of NATO in 1949, the Chinese-Soviet alliance in 1950, and the founding of the Warsaw Pact in 1955 saw the crystallization of the bipolar power dynamic that irreparably divided the East from the West.

CHAPTER 5:
THE NEW AMERICAN EMPIRE

The story of America's rise to the supreme position it found itself in in the 1950s began a little over five decades prior when the young nation first asserted itself on the world stage. They were still stubbornly viewed as something of a backwater by most of the old powers of Europe, but there was no doubt that American power was on the rise. Their industries were fueled by remarkable levels of immigration through the 20th century, which only accelerated when Europe became a war zone both in 1914 and 1939. Still, prior to World War II, nations like France and Britain dominated world affairs, while isolationist America was left as a middling global power. After 1945, with the utter destruction of the old "powers that be," the USSR was indeed the only nation that could challenge the Americans, but in the grand scheme of history, not even they could subdue the political, economic, and sheer military might of the new colossus in the West.

The decline of Europe ushered in the era of a new American Empire, a chapter of history that the world is still living in today.

Global American Occupation

The Truman-led America that emerged after 1945 was not simply capable of bankrolling the economies of an entire continent. It was also capable of exerting military strength in every corner of the war-torn globe. One of the most striking features of this new age was the persistence of American presence in the lands that they had liberated. The Soviets, it seems, were not the only victors of WWII who refused to leave where their armies had stepped. Both during and after the war, Americans began seizing and occupying strategic military bases in the territories they conquered, both in the European and Pacific theaters. They also established brand new bases to house international American soldiers. The occupation of defeated nations, even after peace is signed, is not an entirely new or shocking concept; nations will often maintain troop presence in aggressive nations to ensure that hostilities have ceased and to guarantee the terms of whatever peace treaty has been signed. The American occupation post-1945, however, needs to be understood in the context of Truman's Containment Doctrine. Particularly in the case of Germany and Japan, the Americans were fearful that if their troops left, they would only be replaced by Soviet ones, which would invariably lead to communist scheming.

As American and British troops rolled across Germany from the West, conquering land, they came into possession of many large bases that Hitler had constructed in anticipation of his European assaults. Some of these include the large Panzer Kaserne in Boblingen, built by the Nazis and captured by the Americans in mid-1945. Katterbach

Kaserne, also captured in 1945, served American Air Force units after its seizure. The key feature of these bases, and others, is the fact that the Americans never actually left. Both Panzer Kaserne and Katterbach Kaserne remain active and in service in the US military to this day. The formation of NATO was pivotal in both justifying and enforcing American military presence in post-war Germany and elsewhere and although many of the most important bases were technically under the jurisdiction of international NATO forces, many of them were run and staffed almost exclusively by American personnel. The world knew that Germany was going to be in a dire economic situation once the war was over, and the USSR was already in possession of the majority of eastern Germany, which no one in their right mind believed Stalin would ever relinquish. The situation was ripe for a rise in communist sentiment, and American troops' presence in the country would be effective both in safeguarding against rising communism and against Soviet encroachment into the West.

With the official formation of West Germany, the indefinite American occupation was all but assured. The conditions of the original NATO agreement, which was essentially forced upon the West German government, established the legal framework for allowing American troops to occupy the country at various military bases. There were no clauses that allowed for West Germany to eventually force their removal, nor did West Germany have grounds to appeal their persistent occupation. A similar situation exists in Italy, where the Americans also settle in for the long haul, in places like the Sigonella naval base and the Camp Darby army base in Tirrenia. In the name of continental protection from the evils of Soviet communism, the US was able to massively expand their military reach in these years. Hostile nations were not the only ones subject to this, as both France and Britain also housed huge amounts of American troops. Staggeringly, in 1957, when American presence on the continent was at its peak, there were well over 400,000 pairs of American boots on the ground from the Atlantic coast all the way to the borders of the Iron Curtain (Statista Research Department). The majority of these soldiers, unsurprisingly, were in the contested region of Germany.

In Japan, things were similar, perhaps even more aggressive. After Japanese defeat in the Pacific, the entirety of the home islands came under the direct control of the US Army, led by General Douglas MacArthur, one of the highest-ranking Generals in the entire military. In this position, MacArthur essentially became the military governor of Japan, the ultimate authority that took no direction from Japanese ministers. Seizing power over the islands in September 1945, MacArthur began instituting sweeping reforms in Japanese society, politics, and economy. Japan was geographically close to the USSR, and the Red Army was already present in Korea (formerly occupied by Japan) and was eager to push southward, hungry for a foothold in the home islands. Like in Germany, the potential for communist infiltration was high, and MacArthur and Truman both wanted to ensure that Japan would ultimately rise from the ashes and become a strong, capitalist, and democratic ally, serving as a counterweight against communist influence in the Far East. The detonations of Fat Man and Little Boy did much to prevent further Soviet expansion southward into the home islands, but the Americans couldn't simply leave the country to their own devices, unable to protect against a full Soviet invasion.

The American occupation of Japan was done in phases, and the first order of business was punishment. This was largely handled by the complete demilitarization of the country and by the Tokyo War criminal trials of 1946. After this, it was time to rebuild Japan, create strong capitalist foundations, and safeguard against Soviet influences. In February 1946, American military and civilian representatives drafted a new, democratic constitution for post-war Japan. Japanese input in the creation of the document was almost non-existent, and it was also not optional. The Japanese were forced to accept and adopt the new foundation for their country, which called for the total disbandment of their ground army. It also rendered the Japanese Emperor nothing more than a mere figurehead with no actual executive power. Importantly, it also completely eliminated their right to take up arms for anything other than strict self-defense. A year later, the US established the Far East Command (FECOM), a military organization that created a unified command system in Asia centered on Japan and with MacArthur at the helm. At the time, Mao Tse-Tung's communist rebels were gaining important ground in the war in China, particularly in the north, and FECOM was expected to be an important bulwark against whatever outcome may arise. FECOM also administered and controlled American Army personnel in other occupied territories, like southern Korea and the Philippine Islands.

Officially, the American occupation of Japan ended early, in 1952, but this did not represent reality. Before this, the US compelled Japanese officials to sign and ratify the US-Japan Security Treaty, a document that allowed for thousands upon thousands of American troops to remain in the country, in bases all across the home islands, indefinitely. The Treaty also granted the American military the special right to *directly intervene* in Japanese domestic political affairs. In other words, the Americans granted themselves the exclusive right to militarily intervene in any suspected communist plots on sovereign Japanese land. The only difference between occupation before and after the Security Treaty was that, by a trick of wordplay, American troops were no longer considered "occupation forces." Rather, they were there under the "invitation" of Japan. This fooled exactly no one, as the Japanese were in no position to protest the terms of the Treaty.

There was widespread public opposition to the US-Japan Security Treaty in the years following its signing, particularly between 1959 and 1960, when riots were triggered in response to it. A revised version of the Treaty was signed in 1960, which remains in effect to this day, but the revised version does not necessitate the removal of Americans from Japanese territory. In 1957, FECOM was dismantled, but it was simply replaced with several other smaller US command organizations, one of which was US Army Japan (USARJ), which still exists today. Camp Zama, a military base located in Kanagawa, some 25 miles from Tokyo, serves as the headquarters for USARJ. Yokota Air Base, originally constructed by the Imperial Japanese Military in 1940, today serves as the main base for American air forces in the country, and is home to well over 10,000 American military personnel. Though the Americans accused the Soviets of exerting undue military influence across the world, it seems fair to say that the Americans were just as nefarious in their goal of establishing a new world order according to their own vision.

"Not in my Backyard:" Latin America and Their Good Neighbor to the North

As much as the United States sought to assert itself in far-flung places like Central Europe and East Asia, many believed that the biggest threats to American power may be in their own backyard. Unlike the rest of the world, direct US involvement in Latin America dates back to at least 1898 and even before. That year, an American warship, the USS Maine, exploded while in Cuba's Havana Harbor. Cuba, at the time, was one of the few remaining Spanish colonial possessions in the Americas, and its people had been actively engaged in a revolution there since 1895. The once-invincible Spanish Empire was a shell of its former self, and the Americans knew it. Furthermore, both the American public and government had taken a special interest in the little island of Cuba, believing that it was destined to become a territory of the United States and that it was America's duty as the nation to throw off the shackles of British oppression to also free their brethren in the Caribbean from Spanish chains. So, defeating the Spanish and helping themselves into Spanish territory seemed to be both a simple and desirable task. The explosion of the USS Maine was used as a pretext by the Republic government of William McKinley to directly intervene in the Cuban conflict, thus beginning the Spanish-American War of 1898.

The war was relatively short-lived. Beginning in April, the conflict was over by the end of the year. The Spanish Armada, which once ruled the seas from one edge of the Atlantic to the other, was toppled by the young United States. In the aftermath, the Spanish were forced to abandon Cuba and leave it as an independent state, although it became a new "protectorate" of the United States. The Spanish also surrendered the island of Puerto Rico, which became an American territory. In the Pacific, the island of Guam was given, as was the Philippine archipelago. The year 1898 was one of the most consequential in American and, indeed, world history. It was a sign of the times: The old powers of Europe were waning, and a new juggernaut across the ocean was on the rise. Though it would take several more decades for the United States to truly break apart from the pack, 1898 signaled the death of the Spanish Empire and the birth of the American one.

With American foreign policy, Latin America has always been a special case, entirely separate from Europe, Asia, or elsewhere. Since the Presidency of James Monroe from 1817 to 1825, the so-called Monroe Doctrine has been one of the guiding principles of US policy. The doctrine outlined two separate "spheres" in the world. The first was the Americas, the Western Hemisphere. Monroe asserted that this sphere was the territory of the United States and was firmly under American protection. Colonies that still existed were acknowledged as European possessions, but further European interference anywhere from the northern tip of Canada to the southern tip of Argentina would be considered intolerable. The other sphere was the old world of Europe, the territory of the kings and emperors of old. Monroe and proponents of his doctrine insisted that the conflicts of the Old World were not their conflicts and vowed to avoid interfering in them. This doctrine laid the groundwork for the aggressive American isolationism prior to WWII, which resulted in America only joining at the very end of 1941. In Latin America and the Caribbean, however, the US has been actively pursuing regime changes and government overthrows for years all across the hemisphere.

American involvement in the South has caused a significant rise in anti-American sentiment throughout Latin America since the 1800s, especially in the early 1900s. During the Presidency of FDR, which lasted an astonishing 12 years from 1933 to 1945, America followed his "Good Neighbor" policy, which acknowledged the fact that the US had behaved intolerably toward their southern neighbors in the past and dictated that America should instead pursue peaceful cooperation with the various states of South and Central America. America still involved itself with their domestic affairs during Roosevelt's tenure, but it was a major shift in attitude from 1898. WWII changed all of this. During the war, American officials grew alarmed at the possibility that Nazis and fascists might attempt to reach out to Latin American states and that some of those states may actually be receptive to it, particularly Argentina or Brazil. During the First World War, Mexico was noticeably pro-German, and Germany even attempted to persuade Mexico to pre-emptively attack the US from the south, so the Americans had reason to be wary. Americans had begun to fear that Latin America might actually slip out of their grasp. During the Cold War, this fear was intensified further as rampant poverty throughout Latin America promised fertile ground for the growth of communism and pro-Soviet sentiment.

Under the threat of a communist takeover in America's own backyard, Truman and subsequent administrations reverted foreign policy back to the old imperialistic attitudes of earlier decades. Of course, the Americans felt they needed the legal ability to intervene in the affairs of these nations if they deemed it necessary. To that end, the Inter-American Treaty of Reciprocal Assistance was signed in 1947, with over 20 countries signing on, with the notable exception of Canada, which still had strong ties to Britain and had separate military agreements with the United States. The Treaty outlined a plan for mutual defense of the hemisphere, and more importantly, it gave the US a pretext to meddle in the affairs of its member nations like Mexico, Colombia, and Venezuela. The US was more direct in 1948 with the creation of the Organization of American States (OAS). The United

States had sent George Marshall, the same man behind the Marshall Plan in Europe, to lead an American delegation to Colombia, after which time the OAS was founded. Among the many provisions in the OAS charter, one critical one was that all signatories pledge to actively fight against communist influence, jointly, wherever it may arise in the Americas. In reality, this was a blank check for America to directly intervene in the region whenever they wanted to, so long as it was done under the guise of battling communism.

All of this led to decades of the US supporting brutal, dictatorial regimes throughout Latin America simply because they were effective in fighting communist or even left-wing influences. This included Rafael Trujillo in the Dominican Republic from 1930 to 1961, the Somozas in Nicaragua from 1936 to the late 70s, and Fulgencio Batista in Cuba from 1952 to 1958. The threat of American intervention worked to effectively deter left-wing governments from forming for years, until the early 1950s, when American brute force was demanded in the small nation of Guatemala, directly to the south of Mexico. Prior to 1944, Guatemala was under the boot of the dictator Jorge Ubico, whose government was closely allied to American government and business. In 1944, an uprising caused Ubico to flee the country in a panic, and he was replaced by a man named Juan Arevalo, who sought to liberalize and democratize the country. To this end, he swiftly reintroduced free elections across Guatemala. To help Guatemala's massively impoverished workers and peasants, Arevalo introduced a federal minimum wage and increased access to public education for those families that couldn't afford it.

In the grand scheme of things, Arevalo's reforms were quite mild. Unfortunately, in the bipolar Cold War world, there was little room for nuance or shades of gray. Everything was black or white: democratic or communist, pure or evil, god-fearing or godless. Through this lens, the situation in Guatemala could be seen as nothing other than communist infiltration by Soviet-inspired agents of chaos. Arevalo himself was deemed nothing short of a puppet of the USSR, whose strings spanned across the ocean all the way to Moscow. The US distrusted him to the point of drafting plans to overthrow him. This was in spite of the fact that Arevalo outright denied the possibility of land redistribution. The vast majority of Guatemalan land in the late 1940s and early 1950s was owned by just a few massively wealthy individuals and American corporations, but Arevalo realized that to attempt to seize it and give it to the poor would have been suicide. Why? Because the largest single landowner in Guatemala by far was the New Orleans-based United Fruit Company (UFC), they wielded a tremendous amount of political power in the United States. The UFC, which primarily grew and sold bananas, was also arguably more powerful than the government of Guatemala itself. In 1950, the UFC's profits dwarfed the revenue of Arevalo's entire federal government.

In 1950, Jacobo Arbenz won the Guatemalan presidency in a free and democratic election, replacing Juan Arevalo as leader. Like Arevalo, Arbenz firmly rejected communism and did not seek ties with the USSR, but he was much more liberal than Arevalo was, which alarmed the Truman administration. What made Arbenz particularly dangerous was the fact that he, unlike Arevalo, had committed himself to land reform and the distribution of land to the poor. As was the case with both the USSR in 1917 and communist China in 1949, land reform is often one of the first steps that communist governments take, and the Western world has come to associate land reform with communist takeover. In 1953, Republican Dwight D. Eisenhower, the former Supreme Commander of Allied troops during WWII, won the presidency and replaced Truman's Democrats. Eisenhower was even more staunchly anti-communist than Truman was, and he staffed his government with like-minded people, including the infamous Dulles brothers. John Foster Dulles, a Senator from New York, was promoted to Secretary of State, and his brother Allen Dulles was selected as Director of the CIA. In a testament to the corporate influence and corruption rampant in American politics at the time, the Dulles brothers also just happened to sit on the board of directors at United Fruit and directly profited from the success of the company. Unsurprisingly, they took serious issue with Arbenz's promise to reorganize Guatemalan land.

Arbenz' proposed land reform was very mild compared to those of actual communist governments and only sought to appropriate land that was not being actively used by American corporations. Less than a third of the land in UFC was actually used for banana cultivation, while the rest was held in reserve in case it was needed. The sale of this unused land to peasants was still forbidden by the UFC, and this was what Arbenz wanted to change. None of the profit-generating land was ever under threat, but despite this, the UFC began a massive propaganda smear campaign to paint Arbenz as a radical communist and Soviet puppet that required removal under the terms of the Truman Doctrine. So, in 1953, Eisenhower authorized Operation Success, which was meant to overthrow the Arbenz government via psychological warfare. At the same time, Dulles' CIA began directly funding and training an insurgency force based out of neighboring Honduras. This group was led by a brutal (yet mostly inept) Guatemalan military exile named

Castillo Armas. In June of 1954, Armas' army invaded Guatemala with US permission.

While the insurgents fought in the Honduran border region, the US was staging complex radio hoaxes that were broadcast across the country. These hoaxes told of fantastical and triumphant victories won by the Armas battalion against the Guatemalan army, yet in reality, the Armas men performed terribly and were suffering defeat after defeat at the hands of the army. The CIA also reached out to church leaders across Guatemala's urban areas, who began including anti-government and anti-Arbenz messages in their sermons. The radio hoaxes were the most successful aspects of the campaign, and many Guatemalan soldiers who weren't on the frontlines grew afraid of Armas, who was supposedly steamrolling over their comrades. Many soldiers refused to fight and abandoned their posts. Entire units were disbanded as a result, which allowed Armas to march almost unopposed across the Guatemalan countryside despite his ineffectiveness as a commander.

As a final nail in the coffin, the US began an intense bombing campaign in the nation's capital, Guatemala City, in 1954. The bombs were followed by massive drops of propaganda pamphlets that told of the inevitable victory of Armas' marching forces, meant to scare the residents of the city. Due to the death toll and overall fear in the capital, as well as the fact that it was only a matter of time before Armas reached the city, Arbenz was soon left with no choice but to surrender. On June 27, 1954, Arbenz abdicated from office and later fled the country, clearing the way for the US-supported Armas dictatorship that remained in power until his death three years later. Operation Success was, appropriately enough, a success. At the most basic level, what the Guatemalan operation amounted to was the American overthrow of a popular and democratically elected government in their own backyard and at the behest of a banana company. All this was done in the name of "freedom" from the evils of communism. Clearly, the US was committed to obtaining complete control over the western hemisphere, and the Guatemalan situation marked the beginning of a new and much more aggressive phase of US intervention in Latin America. As we'll see later, American involvement in this region of the world led to the most intense showdown of the entire Cold War.

CHAPTER 6:
THE MIDDLE EAST AND THE ARAB-ISRAELI WARS

The Middle East, a region long dominated by foreign powers from the Ottoman Empire to the British and French, was primed for revolution following the end of WWII. Ethnic groups in the region had been invigorated by a surge in nationalist sentiment, and following the disruption of the European powers' grip throughout the world, many came to believe the time was right to create independent nations of their own and to determine their own destiny. The wider Arab world, which stretched as far as Morocco in western North Africa, was awakening to the reality of the post-war world. At the same time, Europe's Jews, who can trace their lineage back to the Middle Eastern Levant region, were also solidifying their sense of national identity. After the war, after the Holocaust, and after the Nazis were defeated, the question still remained as to what the future held for the world's Jews. Many felt they couldn't stay in a Europe that viewed them as parasites to be eradicated. Like the Arabs, a national homeland was thought to be the answer to the problems of the time. A place where all Jews would be safe, a place where a Holocaust could never again occur, a place where they could defend themselves. Unfortunately, the goals of the Jews and Arabs proved to be irreconcilable, and the homeland the Jews envisioned necessarily involved the disenfranchisement of a people who viewed that future homeland as their own native land.

Zionism and the Balfour Declaration

A prevailing question in history is why exactly Hitler and the Nazi Party initiated the Holocaust. Indeed, not every German hated Jews, and not every Nazi believed that genocide was the answer. Why, then, did Germans resonate so strongly with Nazi ideology? Why was the mass murder seen as an acceptable "final solution"? Although not even all the Nazis believed Europe's Jews were deserving of death, the main cause of the Holocaust was indeed rampant anti-Semitism, not just in Germany but throughout Europe as a whole. By the 1940s, anti-Semitism was already a centuries-old European tradition, and much of it was a result of the Catholic Church. The Vatican had perpetuated the idea that Jewish villainy stemmed from the fact that they were the "killers of Christ," amounting to the ultimate crime against the Christian world. This was despite the fact that, according to Christian doctrine, the death of Jesus was a necessary prerequisite to the forgiveness of humanity's myriad sins. The Church preached about the untrustworthiness of Jews and even claimed, all the way up to the early twentieth century, that Jews were involved in the kidnapping of Christian children, whose blood was used in secret Jewish rituals.

Throughout Europe for centuries, Jews in almost every country were subject to nearly constant persecution. They were limited in what jobs they could hold, and whenever Jewish communities became too prosperous, they were routinely subject to asset seizures by the local or federal governments, whereby their communities were forcibly expelled from the country and had their wealth and property seized. Jews from that community would be dispersed and would have to try to find homes in other European countries as refugees. Especially in Eastern Europe, Jews were also subject to routine pogroms. These were random, sometimes coordinated spasms of violence against their communities, and Jews were often beaten, tortured, and murdered, and their property was destroyed. With no land to call their own, Jews who were forced to leave one country would end up in another, where the cycle of violence and persecution would persist.

In the late 1890s, an Austrian Jew named Theodor Herzl began a movement known as Zionism. Because of the desperate condition of Europe's Jews, Zionism called for the creation of a Jewish homeland where Jews could congregate and determine their own destiny. There were several potential areas that were considered as being the site of a potential homeland, but the most preferable option by far was the traditional Jewish homeland in the Levant (a region that includes modern-day Palestine, Israel, Lebanon, and parts of Syria). For years, Herzl encouraged Jews to migrate to Palestine, which had been under the control of the Ottoman Empire for centuries. Over the years, the ideology of Zionism began to gain a lot of traction, and more and more of those in Europe were making the move to Palestine to join the Jewish community that was already present there, albeit in dwindling numbers. Despite the fact that Jews had been expelled from historical Palestine several times, including by the Assyrians, Babylonians, and

Romans, Herzl preached that the only path to Jewish safety lay in reclaiming territory there.

Anti-Semitism continued for decades, but in 1903, a short book commonly known as *The Protocols of the Elders of Zion* began circulating around Europe, emanating from Russia. Ostensibly, the book contained a secret plan written by Jewish leaders, detailing their intention to dominate global affairs. The book detailed Jewish plans to dominate the press and global economies before enslaving non-Jews and bringing about the end of civilization. The *Protocols*, however, were later proven to be a heavily plagiarized forgery, written by Russians and various other European anti-Semites. By this time, the book had already circulated widely, even reaching America. Even after it was proven to be inauthentic, it was still read widely as a genuine document. Henry Ford, the famous American automaker and virulent anti-Semite, personally circulated the *Protocols* and referenced it directly in his newspaper, the *Dearborn Independent* in the 1920s, long after it was exposed as fiction. The *Protocols* remain the original basis for modern-day claims of Jewish conspiracies.

In 1917, as the First World War raged on and the British were at war with the Ottoman Empire, which had joined the war on Germany's side, the British were forced to contemplate the future of the lands they were conquering from the Ottoman Turks. For years, Jewish groups had been lobbying European governments to gain official state support for the idea of forging a homeland for the Jews. In November 1917, the British government issued the Balfour Declaration, which pledged British support for such a state. It read:

"His Majesty's Government view with favor the establishment in Palestine of a national home for the Jewish people, and will use their best endeavours to facilitate the achievement of this object, it being clearly understood that nothing shall be done which may prejudice the civil and religious rights of existing non-Jewish communities in Palestine, or the rights and political status enjoyed by Jews in any other country," (Yale Law School, The Avalon Project).

Support for the cause was partly due to many in Parliament sympathizing with the historical plight of Europe's Jews. Support also came from the simple fact that many British were happy to be rid of them anyway and would gladly support their migration to somewhere else. Whatever their motivations were, the British had made a historical pledge.

After the end of WWI, Britain occupied portions of former Ottoman land and created the British Mandate for Palestine, with the goal of controlling the area until such time as the people there were deemed ready to govern themselves. In the years leading up to WWII, there was a steady flow of Jewish migrants from Europe into the area to join Jewish communities and build new ones. At the same time, Arabs from across the Arab world were also migrating to Mandatory Palestine, mostly for economic reasons. Arabs and Jews in the region already did not get along exceedingly well historically, and their mutual animosity only grew with the increased migration. Arabs saw Jewish migration as a European colonialist project, while the Jews viewed the Arabs as an impediment to the formation of a Jewish state. The two groups had begun to fight each other for control of the land.

After the end of WWII and the horrors of the Holocaust came to light, much of the world rallied behind the Zionist cause. The only way to prevent another genocide of Jews, a long-stateless people who were considered mere sojourners in Europe, was to form a nation in which they could defend themselves. After 1945, even larger numbers of Jews from Europe, America, and elsewhere flooded into Mandatory Palestine, which soon brought tensions to a boiling point. In 1947, with constant fighting between the region's peoples and with no clear end in sight, the British were eager to abandon the area. The Parliament appealed to the newly-created United Nations for a resolution, and while several ideas were entertained, the only one that had any realistic hope of appeasing both groups was a two-state solution.

1948: The New States of the Middle East

In 1948, as a result of the UN's Resolution 181, the modern states of Israel and Palestine were created. For both Arabs and Jews, nationalist ideology had become intense. Since even before the Ottoman Empire fell, Arabs in the region had come to see themselves not merely as "Arabs" but as ethnic Palestinians with a distinct national heritage. Jews, too, had come to see themselves as Israelis, the rightful occupants of what both they and Muslims considered Holy Land. After the UN Resolution, which split Mandatory Palestine roughly 50/50 (the division of land, both in quality and quantity, was slightly in Israel's favor), the Israelis accepted and immediately declared independence. The Palestinians, many of whom would be forced to abandon their homes and migrate, did not. It was their desire to eradicate the new state of Israel, and in achieving this goal, they were supported by the majority of their Arab neighbors, including Syria, Jordan, and Egypt. Emboldened by their military support, Palestine attacked Israel on May 15, 1948, just one day after Israeli independence. Soon after, each one of Israel's Arab neighbors invaded as well.

The Arab armies greatly outnumbered that of Israel, but in a considerable tactical error, the separate armies did not co-ordinate their attacks, instead staggering their assaults one after another. This meant that the fledgling Israeli military generally had to fight the forces of one nation at a time. In less than a year, the Arab armies were defeated, and Israel gradually signed armistice agreements with their opponents. Over the course of the war, however, the Israeli army had pushed past the UN borders and occupied much of the land that was destined to become Palestine. The only portions that remained out of Israeli control were the West Bank, which came under control of Jordan, and the Gaza Strip, which Egypt controlled. In the process of seizing nearly 80% of the former British Mandate, massive numbers of Palestinians were attacked and expelled in order to make room for Jewish settlers. The new state of Israel, despite being attacked, was harshly criticized for this, as well as their use of biological warfare—in some areas, local water supplies were purposefully contaminated to prevent Palestinians from returning to their villages. The global backlash against Israel led to increased violence against Jews across the Arab world, which only increased Jewish migration to the Levant. Palestinians, of course, never accepted the defeat of 1948 and continued to attack Israel for years, setting the stage for a decades-long conflict.

In the years leading up to 1967, Palestinian attacks against Israeli civilians increased dramatically, which led to brutal Israeli retaliation, which also targeted Palestinian civilians. While this was happening, Israel's neighbors were once again mobilizing their land armies and preparing for another war. Egypt had blockaded Israeli ports, and Iraq had begun preparing an invasion force. To gain the upper hand, Israel attacked first on June 5, 1967. Thanks to significant military assistance from the West, the war was a complete rout. The advanced Israeli air force decimated Egypt's ground troops, and their land army had pushed well into Egyptian territory, conquering both the Gaza Strip and the entirety of the Sinai peninsula, the latter of which guaranteed that Egypt could no longer blockade Israel's ports. To the north, Israel had also pushed into Syria and seized the Golan Heights, an area from which Syria had launched attacks against Israel. In what became known as the Six-Day War, Israel claimed victory on June 10 and ceased the advancement of their troops. Casualties in the war were very disproportionate, especially in the case of Egypt, which had lost over 10,000 soldiers. Israel, in comparison, had suffered only around 900 deaths.

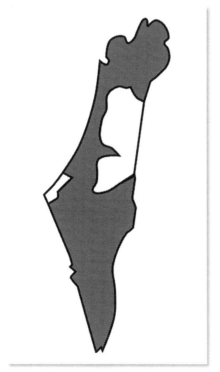

The division of Palestinian land after the Arab-Israeli Wars. The largest portion is Israel, and the two smaller portions make up Palestine. The western portion is Gaza, and the eastern portion is the West Bank.

Again, Israel gradually made peace with its neighbors, exchanging some of the land they had conquered in exchange for guarantees that they would no longer be attacked. This included Egypt's Sinai Peninsula, which Israel gave back after the brief 1973 Yom Kippur War. The peace was met with outrage in Egypt, particularly among extremist groups, and Egyptian President and Nobel Peace Prize winner Anwar el-Sadat was assassinated in 1981, partly due to his desire to create and maintain peace with the Israeli state. While a fragile peace was established between Israel and her neighbors following 1967, peace with the Palestinian people was never truly achieved. After 1967, Israel had come to occupy the *entirety* of Mandatory Palestine, leaving the Palestinians without any land in which to call home and leaving the task of governing the Palestinians to the Israeli state, a government that had been antagonistic toward them for decades. Sectarian violence continued to grow and occasionally erupted into armed conflict, but the specter of the Arab-Israeli conflict remains powerful to this day. The 1948 and 1967 wars are just a few of the wider impacts of Western influence in the Middle East, the influence that has done much to irreparably damage that region of the globe. Many continue to see the Arab-Israeli conflict as a symptom of the wider Cold War struggle between the USA and USSR—many of the Arab states had been supported by the Soviets, who had come to view Israel as a mere puppet of the United States. Given the seemingly endless support for Israel given by the American government, this point is hard to contest. In any case, the wars and violence that have plagued both the Palestinian and Israeli people must be understood in the context of the post-WWII political climate that has consumed the world in these years.

CHAPTER 7:
REVOLUTION AND DECOLONIZATION

After WWII, the Middle East wasn't the only region where European interests became disrupted and fractured. Across the world, from Africa to Asia, lands formerly belonging to European colonial empires had begun to cry for freedom and self-determination. Nationalist sentiment was on the rise, and with it came the spirit and determination to win independence by whatever means necessary. To many colonized people, hearing European leaders preach about the virtues of freedom, liberty, and self-determination during the Second World War was the epitome of hypocrisy. They spoke of the threat of foreign domination by the Germans, the Italians, or the Japanese, at the same time that they willingly subjugated other people who they still believed to be racially inferior to themselves. Thus, the desire to dismantle European colonial holdings grew, both within Europe and in the colonized lands. Although the decolonization process would take decades to complete, the years after 1945 saw the solidification of a national consciousness for countless of the world's oppressed.

Algeria, Ethiopia, and the New States of Africa

In August 1941, just months before the United States entered WWII, Franklin D. Roosevelt and Winston Churchill convened to hold preliminary talks about what the post-war world might look like. The document that was produced as a result of these talks was known as the Atlantic Charter, and largely because of Roosevelt's insistence, the Charter called for supporting the self-determination of peoples that had been denied it historically. The document also called for widespread free elections in the post-war world to ensure that these free people also had their choice in the governing system (i.e., it would not be determined for them by the victors). Unfortunately, it was clear from Churchill's later actions that he interpreted this declaration as applying only to European territory and not to the colonial territories Britain held across the world. Roosevelt, unlike most of his contemporaries, including his Vice President and successor, envisioned this as a guide for the entire world.

Since the beginning of the so-called "Scramble for Africa" in the 1870s, nearly every square inch of that continent has been claimed and colonized by various European powers. Home to thousands of diverse ethnic groups, "tribalism" has often been considered the bane of Africa. For countless years, ethnic conflict had prevented any kind of long-term African unity or solidarity and thus prevented the formation of united coalitions against European colonialism. European powers had effectively turned African groups against each other for their own benefit; however, during the war, African colonial groups were forced to fight alongside each other, regardless of tribe, for a common cause and purpose. Young men and women, who for so long had seen each other as the opponents under European yoke, had now come to understand and empathize with one another. The development of African nationalism was beginning to form. The war as a whole showed them that it was possible, indeed desirable, to band together to overcome a common enemy. In their case, their common enemy was their colonial overlords, who had stripped their land of resources and their people of dignity for generations. In later years, regions like Nigeria (formerly British) and Somalia (formerly British and Italian) gained their independence through largely peaceful strategies that utilized nationalist ideologies to garner the support of the people, but in the African regions where most of the fighting during the war had taken place, including North Africa and the Horn of Africa, the situations were different.

The Ethiopian Empire, which lay in the Horn of Africa region across the Dead Sea from the Gulf of Arabia, was the last African kingdom to be conquered by a European power. Throughout its history, Ethiopia, formerly known as Abyssinia, was a powerful state, and when the Italians invaded them in the 1890s, the Ethiopians were able to soundly drive them back out of Africa with their superior weaponry. The fact that a European society had been militarily defeated by an African one flew in the face of the European idea that other races were inherently inferior to them. The terrible loss dealt to them by the Ethiopians remained a source of embarrassment for the Italians for years leading up to the Second World War, and after the rise of fascist dictator Benito Mussolini in 1922, it became the object of obsession for the military. It was a wrong that needed correction, and in 1935, they invaded again. This time, the Italians were victorious, Ethiopian

Emperor Haile Selassie was forced into exile, and Mussolini was able to add to his country's colonial holdings in Africa.

By 1942, as the Second World War raged on, the combined Ethiopian and British forces had forced the Italian fascists out of Ethiopia entirely as the Italian war machine crumbled under the weight of its own outdated and cumbersome machinery. The Italian defeat at the Battle of Gondar in late November 1941 marked the end of the effective Italian occupation of Ethiopia, and with this triumph came the question of what was to become of the liberated land. Surely, giving it back to Italy was out of the question. Perhaps subjugating the land under British "protection" for the foreseeable future would have been preferable, but given the strength of Ethiopian resistance, this could have been disastrous. Negotiations over control of the land began sometime after the Italians had been ousted in an effort to re-establish Ethiopian independence and reinstall Emperor Selassie, a member of the centuries-old Solomonid Dynasty. The original agreement that was drawn up between the British and Ethiopians involved granting the British various important privileges and concessions in the region, but after heavy lobbying by the Ethiopians, the British soon surrendered most of these terms. The revised treaty that came to be known as the Anglo-Ethiopian Agreement was signed in late 1944, and the last African kingdom to be conquered had won its independence once again.

North Africa, home to the modern-day nations of Morocco, Algeria, Tunisia, Libya, and Egypt, was one of the main theaters of battle during the Second World War. Although the arid deserts of the southern Mediterranean coasts have often been considered peripheral battlefields in comparison to Europe or the Pacific, some of the most consequential battles of the entire war took place here. The western territories of Algeria, Tunisia, and most of Morocco had been under the control of France for decades, and while Egypt to the East had been independent since 1922, that country was still largely influenced and controlled by the British Empire. The land in between, which comprises modern-day Libya, was a possession of the Nazi-allied Italians, and it was from here that the Axis launched their attacks against Allied colonial lands in the area. After the war, and after Axis forces had been completely driven out of North Africa and back into Italy and beyond, it was up to the victorious allies and the United Nations to determine the future course for North Africa. At first, the now Mussolini-less Italian government maintained control of their holdings across the Mediterranean, but the mandate from the UN General Assembly after the war called for the total independence of all land formerly owned by the Fascist Italian state.

In the coming years, the Libyan regions of coastal Tripolitania, Egypt-adjacent Cyrenaica, and land-locked Fezzan were all released from Italian rule, and in 1951, they united under a single banner, the United Kingdom of Libya under King Idris As-Senussi. For years prior to the war, Mussolini and his government had encouraged Italians to migrate to and settle in North Africa as a way to solidify Libya as a core part of the Italian homeland. By the time WWII broke out, Italians with permanent residence in Libya had numbered well over 100,000, the majority of whom remained a major demographic in Libya even after independence in 1951. It wasn't until the rule of Muammar Gaddafi in the 1970s that a mass exodus of the remaining Italians took place. Their forced exile by the Gaddafi government was driven by the assertion that, as was the case in many former colonial lands, foreign peoples were still dominating and exploiting Libya. Tens of thousands of settlers were banished from the country, and in the years and decades following, their numbers dwindled to almost nothing.

Around the same time that Libya had gained its independence from Italy, French North Africa was becoming a major problem for the government of French President Vincent Auriol. By 1954, their colonies there, including Algeria, Morocco, and Tunisia, were astir, with revolts being sparked in all three regions that year. While Morocco and Tunisia maintained some nominal independence as "protectorates" of France, Algeria was always a unique case. Algeria had been incorporated as a core part of France, just as the Italians tried to do in Libya. The French settlement of Algerian land was extensive, and at its height, there were over 1.5 million French settlers who received special treatment from the Franco-Algerian government there. Surrendering Morocco and Tunisia would be a loss, but losing Algeria could have been disastrous for the French living there, most of whom would be forced to return to France, whose cities were already overpopulated and struggling to rebuild after the horrors of the war. In 1956, amid the rampant civil unrest, the French fully released both Morocco and Tunisia as independent nations, largely in order to focus fully on the problem of retaining Algeria.

The Algerian rebels, who were fighting to rid the country of French influence, were heavily supported and directly funded by the Egyptian government of newly-elected Gamal Abdel Nasser. Nasser had risen to prominence on a platform of Arab unity and solidarity against foreign powers, and his pan-Arab government publicly supported the independence of all Arab Muslim states, including Algeria. Knowing the Algerian rebels were being propped up by the agitator Nasser, the

French then undertook to destabilize Egypt and their government in order to cripple the resistance. The French weren't alone in their demonization of Egypt. In the summer of 1956, Nasser made the unilateral decision to nationalize the Suez Canal, a man-made channel in Egypt that runs through Egypt, connecting the Mediterranean and Red Seas and separating the Sinai Peninsula from the rest of Egypt. It's one of the most important routes for trade in the world, and since its construction in the 1860s, it has been run jointly by the British and French. Being the only sea route to Asia that did not require sailing around the entire continent of Africa, losing control over Suez was intolerable, particularly to the British. Soon after this news, the British and French joined forces in a joint effort to destroy Nasser and his government and to reclaim European control of Suez.

In October 1956, the combined French, British, and Israeli forces attacked and invaded Egypt. The Egyptian Army was plagued with incompetence at its highest levels, largely because there were still many top generals who had won their positions due to political connections rather than military capability. As it turns out, though, the military skill of either side did not matter much in the grand scheme of the invasion. The conflict had threatened to develop into a larger conflict in the context of the Cold War because Egypt was supported by the USSR while the Americans had a vested interest in supporting Britain, France, and particularly Israel. Because the French-British-Israeli alliance had taken major offensive action without the approval of the new leaders of the Eastern and Western blocs, both the USA and USSR were extremely dissatisfied with the invasion. The Soviets rebuked Egypt's enemies, and the United States heavily pressured them to cease their invasion. As a result of this international lobbying, the invaders were forced to stand down, and their troops were withdrawn from the country to be replaced by UN troops to ensure peaceful relations. Egypt had suffered a military defeat, but ultimately, control of the Suez remained in their hands. The Suez Crisis, as it came to be known, was a major indication of the new world order that was to be. For the first time, major European powers were bending to the will of the United States, retreating with their tails between their legs after being chastised for daring to undertake military action without the express approval of the Americans. The days of Europeans independently dictating world events, or even their own destinies were largely over.

By 1956, the eventual dissolution of Europe's overseas empires was a foregone conclusion. In later years, French Prime Minister Charles de Gaulle would make several admissions that foreshadowed this end. The efforts that France had expended in maintaining colonial control, he argued, had actually severely weakened the French homeland. In struggling to hold onto what was inevitably slipping from their grasp, France was left completely unable to keep up with the technological advances that were being enjoyed by the United States and the USSR. So, de Gaulle and the French set out to address the number one colonial headache they had on their hands: Algeria. Negotiations with the rebels were opened, and in 1962, the Algerians had won their independence from France. The French that had settled in Algeria were forcibly deported and sent back across the Mediterranean. By this point, North Africa and the Horn of Africa were entirely different places from when WWII began, and West African nations like Nigeria were also beginning to throw off the shackles of colonialism and forge their own path forward. While the war had been destructive for the nations of Europe, their former colonial lands had reached a new renaissance.

The Chinese Civil War and the Rise of Asian Communism

After 1945, important events and developments occurred each day, and while some were encouraging the new American superpower, many were startling. The Soviet Union's bellicose attitude toward Eastern Europe, the rise of socialist-leaning political leaders in Latin America, and the communist-tinged revolutionary groups that were forming in former European colonial lands across the world were all cause for raised eyebrows in the Truman and Eisenhower administrations. However, perhaps the most worrisome case in the immediate post-war years was China. Beginning in 1927, China had become embroiled in a bloody civil war between the right-wing nationalist government, the Kuomintang (KMT), and left-wing communists across the country. The KMT was led by the brutal General Chiang Kai-shek, and the largest and most well-equipped communist group, the Chinese Communist Party (CCP), was led by the charismatic revolutionary Mao Tse-Tung.

A Map of Chinese Provinces.

The KMT and the CCP had been at war with each other intermittently for years, but the situation changed drastically in the 1930s. Years prior to the outbreak of WWII in Europe, East Asia was already being torn apart. The Imperial Japanese Army had been running wild through the Pacific, conquering their Asian neighbors in order to create a Japanese sphere of dominance in the East. By the late 1930s, Japan was already in control of all of Korea and had been expanding across Manchuria. In 1937, the Japanese officially invaded mainland northern China in what would become easily one of the bloodiest theaters of the entire Second World War. Unfortunately for the invaders, the KMT and CCP had come to an understanding that neither side could pursue their vision for the country if China was reduced to a mere puppet of the Japanese. So Mao and Chiang joined together, forming a United Front against the invaders.

Important gains were made across China by the Japanese, and terrible atrocities against their people followed, but against the combined strength of the Chinese military and the communist guerrillas, Imperial Japan couldn't prevail. As the nationalist army waged traditional warfare against the Japanese, the communists complemented it with extensive guerrilla tactics, including sabotage, ambush, and hit-and-run attacks. At the same time, the demands of the Second World War had spread Japan's forces thin, with campaigns taking place in Indochina, the Philippines, the Dutch East Indies, Thailand, and across the Pacific islands. The downturn of Japan's forces against the United States matched their fortunes against China, and after decisive victories by Mao's forces, the Japanese invasion was doomed. By the end of 1945, the Imperial Army had been fully flushed out of mainland China as well as Taiwan, an island off the coast of China that had been granted back to the Kai-shek government.

With the triumph over Emperor Hirohito's forces, the Chinese Civil War was set to begin anew. Since the formation of the United Front, however, the administration of Kai-shek's KMT has become bloated, corrupt, and ineffective. Nationalist forces had been significantly weakened, and Mao had publicly mocked and criticized the KMT's laziness in the war against Japan, choosing to defend the territory they held rather than fight for the country's total liberation as the communists had done. Meanwhile, as support for the KMT waned, Mao and the CCP won widespread popular support, particularly among the peasantry that dominated China's massive countryside. It was clear that the Nationalists were on the losing side of the public relations battle, and in the years immediately following WWII, the KMT made repeated attempts at outreach to establish peace. Mao and the CCP were open to this, but random and uncontrollable spasms of violence across the frontlines prevented talks from progressing.

By the middle of 1947, the civil war was back in full swing, and the incompetent KMT leadership could not keep up with the vast popularity that Mao enjoyed. The communists were winning victory after victory and picking up a parade of new rural and urban supporters along the way. By 1948, Kai-shek's Nationalists were fully on the defensive and losing badly. Much of the fighting was taking place in Northern China and Manchuria, and the forces of the KMT were steadily being pushed southward and toward the coast. As they retreated, many KMT officials and soldiers began defecting to Mao's communist forces, further bolstering their numbers and worsening Kai-shek's position. By 1948, the CCP was in control of over a third of all

Chinese territory and had massive peasant support, and as they pushed closer to heavily populated areas, they began winning the support of the middle classes and urban working-class poor as well. The CCP, once much smaller than the KMT government army, was now better equipped and commanded a much larger force than their enemies.

To compound Kai-shek's misfortunes, the KMT had since 1945 been steadily but severely inflating their currency, the Chinese Yuan, triggering a steep economic decline. The Yuan was debased, and the Chinese economy soon imploded as the country teetered into bankruptcy. Tens of millions of Chinese were left financially damaged, if not destitute. Millions of newly poor urban dwellers began to look to Mao's communist policies to provide a better economic system than the one that had just brought the country to ruin. While the citizens of Chinese cities floundered across the country, the KMT had made no effort to assuage their pain. Meanwhile, they had been hearing stories of Mao's outreach to the rural peasantry and their efforts to establish democratic rule in areas long dominated by feudalism and slave-like labor tenancy. The CCP had made it a primary goal to abolish massive land ownership and to redistribute land to the peasants as a safeguard against impoverishment. These goals resonated massively with the most downtrodden Chinese, as did Mao's aggressive vengeance against those who had been exploiting the poor for decades. As he said in April 1948:

> "We consider it absolutely necessary and proper to sentence to death, through the people's courts and the democratic governments, those major criminals who have actively and desperately opposed the people's democratic revolution and sabotaged the land reform, that is, the most heinous counter-revolutionaries and local tyrants.

If this were not done, democratic order could not be established," (Selected Works of Mao Tse-tung, April 1, 1948, marxists.org).

Chinese workers had already cast their lot with Mao, and the nationalists were on the run. After a long string of victories in 1949, the communists had won and the KMT was forced to flee mainland China, almost all of which was under CCP control, and sail to Taiwan, the small island off the coast of China that Japan had surrendered after 1945. The KMT took along with them a few million refugees (many rich landowners and industry leaders whose executions Mao had advocated for) as well as a massive portion of China's gold reserves and currency. The KMT then established a kind of government-in-exile on the island, and to this day, the KMT is the ruling party of Taiwan, a nation that insists it's the "true" China.

On October 1, 1949, Mao proclaimed the independence of the new People's Republic of China. The long-fought Chinese Revolution and the resounding success of the Communist Party sent massive shockwaves throughout Asia, particularly Vietnam and Korea, as we'll see. The Western world, too, felt the reverberations echoing from China, as Mao's victory represented what many leaders in America had come to see as their worst nightmare. The international forces of communism now had a major new ally, a possible juggernaut in Asia that wielded the potential to command massive economic power, given its staggeringly large population. The news was taken with much more optimism in the USSR. Initially, Stalin was pleased with the CCP's victory and publicly congratulated Mao for supposedly liberating the workers of China and banishing the authoritarian KMT from the country. After all, Stalin and the entire Soviet government had been eagerly awaiting the day that another major nation adopted communism *without* the direct intervention of the USSR. The following year, in 1950, the Chinese and Soviets signed the Sino-Soviet Treaty of Friendship, Alliance, and Mutual Assistance, which outlined an alliance between the two major nations and provided for aid to be sent to the fledgling CCP from the USSR. More importantly, though, the treaty marked the beginning of a new and frightening stage of the Cold War. The Americans and their Western allies were now up against the combined forces of Stalin and Mao, a united front against the capitalist democracies of America and Western Europe. American leaders, including President Truman, were distressed, but the Chinese Revolution was only the latest in what would be a streak of misery in Asia.

A Chinese postage stamp from 1950 depicting the friendship between Stalin and Mao

Unrest in Asia: India and the First Indochina War

In the 1930s, European powers were in control of vast amounts of land in Asia and the Pacific. The Dutch controlled a huge portion of Indonesia, the British controlled parts of Malaysia and Burma as well as India, and the French controlled Indochina, a region that consists of modern-day Laos, Cambodia, and Vietnam. In the years following the surprise Japanese assault on Pearl Harbor in 1941 (which included simultaneous attacks across the Pacific), the Japanese Empire conquered virtually all of this colonial land. In short order, the Japanese had invaded and conquered Burma, Malaysia, Siam (modern-day Thailand), the Dutch East Indies, the Philippines, as well as French Vietnam, Cambodia, and Laos. In the process of seizing this territory, the Japanese had severely crippled, if not utterly destroyed, the European colonial systems as well as their economic systems. This had undermined the long-standing European presence in Asia, perhaps irreparably. Worse, as had happened in Africa and elsewhere, the war had forced the people of Asia to seriously reconsider their relationship with Europe. Colonialism, obviously, had always been an unpopular and unenjoyable experience for the colonized, but along with WWII came three important realizations. First, considering the humiliation that the Europeans endured at the hands of the Japanese in the Pacific Theater, being a colony clearly did not necessarily mean that they would be protected. The long-standing myth of white superiority had been smashed after the British fled before the superior firepower and discipline of the Japanese. Second, their European overlords weren't nearly as powerful in the late 1930s as they had believed. Third and most importantly, social and political change was possible, and their colonial overlords could be overthrown.

Just like in Palestine, religious and ethnic strife were also major considerations in the Asian colonies. This was particularly true in India (referred to as the British Raj), the so-called "crown jewel" of the British Empire and its proudest colonial possession. During WWII, Indian soldiers were vital to the British efforts in the Pacific, and the massive population of India meant that they were able to field a considerable number of troops. Besides defending their homeland, Indian troops were present in the fight for Burma, Sri Lanka (then known as Ceylon), as well as in the streets of Europe against the Nazis and the deserts of North Africa. Their involvement had left the Indian armed forces with a wealth of experience as well as the skills to wage modern war. Plus, after 1945, the Indian subcontinent was well-positioned to become a potential industrial and economic powerhouse. Given its population, natural resources, and industries, India was perhaps better suited than ever before to create an economy that could dwarf the majority of the rest of Asia. Since the 1930s, various Indian groups have been working to create a representative government for India that would put the needs of Indians, not British, first. This was the first step in what many believed to be the ultimate path to complete independence. After 1945, this fight was greatly accelerated.

Unfortunately, Indian society had long been strictly divided along religious-ethnic lines, and there were long and bitter tensions between the majority of Hindus and the Muslim Indians who lived predominantly in the north of the country. Two opposing political factions had risen to dominate the campaign for Indian independence: The Congress Party and the Muslim League. The Congress Party was generally a secular organization, but its leadership was undoubtedly dominated by Hindus, and they resented the fact that India was dragged into the broader conflict of WWII by the empire without any acknowledgment of Indian interests. The Muslim League, of course, was a strictly Muslim organization that advocated for the protection of Muslim rights in the country and for the establishment of a separate

Muslim society within the borders of the British Raj. Through the later years of the war, the Muslim League exploded in popularity in the Islamic sections of India.

It quickly became clear that the Indian people and the political groups representing them did not simply want independence from Britain. The only clear answer was the creation of two separate states, one for the Hindus and another for the Muslims. In 1946, several events happened that pushed India and its people toward this goal. The large Indian army had been openly revolting against the British officers that commanded their units, and in February, the Indian Royal Navy famously mutinied and caused significant damage to the British hold on the Indian military. In the space of just two days, control of the vast majority of its navy had shifted into the hands of the revolters. Eventually, the mutiny was put down, largely due to a lack of support from India's two premiere parties, but the message had been sent: Britain's crown jewel was slipping away. In the summer, the large eastern city of Calcutta, home to a large and diverse population of Muslims, Hindus, and Sikhs, exploded in violent riots characterized by ethnic attacks between Hindus and Muslims. By the time the violence was quelled, thousands had been killed, and over 15,000 Indians had been injured. It became clear to the British that, in the absence of independence, a civil war would be imminent, one that Britain would have the ultimate responsibility for handling. Britain was a nation in desperate need of time to repair itself, and the prospect of having to clean up the bloody civil war of a nation whose population dwarfed its own was too difficult to bear. All sides quickly realized that negotiation was the best course of action for the future of India.

On February 20, 1947, Britain's new Labour Party Prime Minister Clement Attlee announced the British plan to hand over the governorship of the British Raj to the Indian people themselves:

"His Majesty's government wish to make it clear that it is their definite intention to take the necessary steps to effect the transference of power into responsible Indian hands by a date not later than June, 1948. . .It is important that the efficiency of civil administration be maintained and the defense of India provided for" (United Press International archives, February 20, 1947.

Even with this declaration of Britain's intentions, civil war in India still appeared to be rapidly approaching. In an effort to avoid this, Attlee's government began negotiations with both the Congress Party and the Muslim League. Realistically, there was only ever one workable solution, and it was a foregone conclusion: partition. On July 18, 1947, the Indian Independence Act received Royal Assent in Parliament, and the British soldiers and civilians were shipped back home. By mid-August, the British Raj was no more, and India and Pakistan had become the newest countries to win their liberty from a European colonizer. The new nation of India was granted the vast majority of the peninsula of India, which includes all of the southern and central regions. Pakistan, the nation granted to the British Raj's large Muslim population, consisted of two separate regions, one in the northwest and the other in the northeast. The northwestern portion eventually consisted of all of Gwadar and Kalat provinces, as well as a portion of Punjab. Northeastern Pakistan on the opposite side of India consisted of a large portion of Bengal, a region that in the 1970s would become the modern-day nation of Bangladesh.

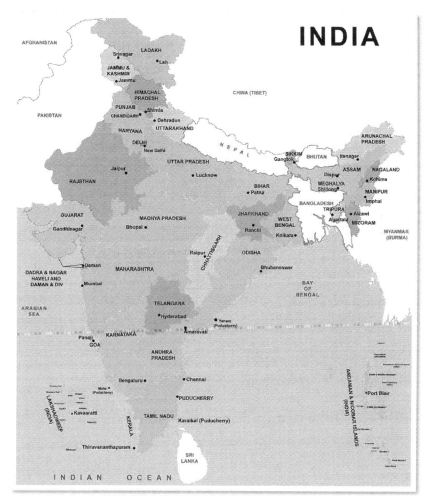

A map of modern-day India after partition, including Pakistan in the northwest and Bangladesh (formerly East Pakistan) in the northeast.

Just like with the partitions of Germany, Palestine, and elsewhere, the splitting of the country involved extensive, sometimes forced relocation of civilians. Many Muslims who found themselves living in Hindu-majority areas near Pakistan, and vice versa, were forced to flee across the border to avoid ethnically-motivated violence in the wake of independence. British possession of the Indian subcontinent had come to an end, and two independent states had risen from the ashes of its rule. But, even with independence, the tensions in the northern regions of the country did not disappear. To this day, there remains contested territory in the north and both India and Pakistan claim it as their own. This is particularly true in the Kashmir region in the extreme north of the subcontinent, where Sikhs also lay claim. There have been frequent outbursts of violence in the border regions, and several wars have plagued the region, especially Kashmir. Acts of terrorism across the border have been common for decades, and since both India and Pakistan became nuclear-armed powers in later decades, the continued threat of war has become far more menacing.

To a large extent, the current situation in India since 1947 is a direct result of the Second World War and Britain's inability to administer their colonies effectively after the destruction that the war caused across both Europe and Asia. The British Empire had proven itself to be very much imperfect and the illusion of British dominance had vanished before the eyes of Indians everywhere. The extensive loss of their territory was a sign of changing times, but India was by far their proudest possession. The inability of what was once the largest empire on earth to retain their most valued asset was the most significant marker that the era of British colonial dominance was over. It wasn't the last, however.

Unlike India, the territory of British Burma, which lay to the east of India across the Bay of Bengal, had been completely overrun by the Japanese Imperial Army during WWII. As the Japanese pushed into Burma from neighboring Japanese-occupied Thailand, the structures of the pre-war British colonial administration were steadily eroded and eventually destroyed altogether. The system that Britain had built up over the decades was in ruins, and the Japanese worked to replace it with their own form of imperial rule. Before this could happen, though, WWII was coming to a close, and the Japanese were retreating from the country back to their home islands. This left Burma in a kind of state of limbo, where no foreign nation had the capacity to effectively run the government, and if the British hoped to regain their prior level of control, it would require massive investments of time and resources, neither of which could be readily afforded. The path to independence was being paved.

In 1939, at the outbreak of the war, the situation in Burma had already become grim. That August, Burmese independence leader Aung San founded the Communist Party of Burma (CPB), a startling development that led many in Britain and America to worry that they might ally themselves with Stalin or Mao's communist forces in nearby China. Surprisingly, though, it was the Japanese that approached him and his party with a tempting offer. In exchange for the cooperation of the CPB, Japan would send relief and military aid to Burma, as well as help train Burmese fighters. Seeing few alternatives to secure a free Burma, Aung San reluctantly agreed, and the CPB made a deal with the devil. When the Japanese invaded Burma in 1942, their forces were greatly aided by Aung San's military, but as the invasion dragged on, the communists started to worry that either way, they would end up being dominated by the British or by the Japanese, both of which were unacceptable for their nationalist aspirations. If they continued to assist the Imperial Japanese Army in conquering Burma, it was very likely that the Japanese would simply never leave. In 1944, as it appeared more and more likely that the Japanese were going to lose the war anyway, Aung San forsook his tenuous alliance with the Japanese, allying instead with the British and Americans. The CPB also began a secret discussion with the Burma National Army to form a united front against Japan's occupation. The result was the formation of the Anti-Fascist Organization, which in 1945 morphed into the Anti-Fascist People's Freedom League (AFPFL).

Fighting raged on, and by mid-1945, the Japanese occupation was crumbling and the Imperial Army had been forced out of Burma entirely. Although the AFPFL was aided in its goal by British colonial troops, anti-British sentiment remained incredibly high after the war. Considering Aung San's incredible popularity and military control, the British quickly realized they wouldn't have the resources to prevent a war of independence for long. With that, they began negotiations with Aung San in 1946 to bring about a peaceful end to British rule, and in 1947, an agreement was reached that assured Burma's independence. By this time, Aung San had distanced himself from the Burmese communists, and when elections were held in 1947, his AFPFL won in a landslide, with the CPB finishing a distant second in the popular vote. In October, the Anglo-Burmese Treaty was signed, and independence was declared in 1948. Unfortunately, Aung San, the father of Burmese independence, did not live to see it. In July 1947, armed gunmen burst into a meeting held by Aung San and unleashed full clips of automatic weapons, killing him and several in his cabinet.

Vietnam, Cambodia, and Laos, collectively referred to as Indochina, had been a colonial possession of France since the 1880s. Indochina was further east of Burma, so the war's effects were felt there much sooner, especially considering their French overlords had been completely conquered by the Germans in a matter of weeks. In June

1940, France surrendered to the invading Nazi forces, and the majority of their colonial lands came under the control of so-called Vichy France, a puppet state of Germany helmed by the Nazi-sympathizing Philippe Petain. Barely three months later, in September, Japanese forces launched an invasion into French Indochina in order to seal off China's southern border and choke out the Chinese resistance forces. The invasion was mostly unsanctioned, as Vichy France and Japan were now technically allies, but a brief conflict broke out that lasted about 4 days. In that time, Japan was able to take control of Vietnam, Cambodia, and Laos and station Imperial Japanese troops there. In 1941, during the occupation, a man named Ho Chi Minh returned to his native Vietnam from a long trip overseas, where he had visited France, America, China, the USSR, and elsewhere. Ho was a well-known figure, not just in Vietnam but in communist circles around the world. He was a revolutionary and his return to Vietnam was one of the most important moments in the nation's history.

In plain terms, Ho returned to Vietnam with the goal of winning complete independence for his homeland as well as establishing a communist Vietnamese state in place of the colonial government. Ho and the other Vietnamese communists had long been opposed to French rule, and with the invasion of another Asian power, many believed that the Japanese would act as liberators. When that illusion was shattered, their new main enemy became the Japanese invaders. Ho formed the Viet Minh, a guerilla military force that began attacking the Japanese both in northern Vietnam and southern China. These guerilla operations dragged on for years until the Japanese oil reserves had run dry and their war machine began to seize up and crumble across the Pacific. Finally, the Japanese forces in Indochina were defeated and forced to retreat in 1945. The newest invaders were gone, but the old ones were soon to return. The newly liberated French were now eager to reclaim their Asian colonies. Ho and the Viet Minh, however, refused to allow Vietnam to return to colonial statehood under the French foreigners who had oppressed their people.

To this end, Ho Chi Minh officially announced Vietnam's independence in September 1945 and the creation of the Democratic Republic of Vietnam. Needless to say, the French did not accept this. Troops were sent to Vietnam, occupied the southern part of the country relatively quickly, and began attacking the communist revolutionaries, whose base of power was in the north near the border with China. Limited negotiations were attempted early on, but by 1946, these had completely broken down and war had erupted between the French-occupied south and the Viet Minh-occupied north. This became known as the First Indochina War, a bloody conflict that raged on until 1954.

The French proved far less willing to surrender their pre-war colonies than the British had been. French troops fought aggressively against the northern communists, but admittedly, the guerilla tactics of the Viet Minh were difficult to overcome. In addition to the skilled strategies of the North Vietnamese Army, they had also been receiving support from Mao's forces in China for years, even before the victory of the CCP in the civil war. After Mao emerged victorious in 1949 and came under the control of all of mainland China, Ho Chi Minh's power in Vietnam was significantly boosted. He now had an ideological ally with a shockingly large military force right on his northern border. Over the 7 years of conflict, the Chinese communists sent millions of units of guns, artillery, bullets, bombs, food, medicine, and various other necessities to northern Vietnam to aid the war. In a show of communist solidarity, both communist China and the USSR sent significant monetary aid to the country in order to help the Viet Minh rebuild Vietnamese infrastructure and stimulate their economies. The tide was turning against the French, and across the ocean, the American administrations of both Truman and Eisenhower were watching closely with a worried gaze.

In March of 1954, a large contingent of French troops were holed up at Dien Bien Phu, a town in the extreme northwest of Vietnam where the French created a stronghold. The Viet Minh, in anticipation of launching a massive siege against the French there, had carved tunnels into the nearby mountains, from which they were able to place artillery that they could quickly pull back into the mountain to keep safe from return fire. Under the leadership of Vietnamese General Vo Nguyen Giap, the Vietnamese assault was fierce. The siege on Dien Bien Phu was long, lasting until early May, and the French were unable to do anything against the Vietnamese barrage. Finally, on May 7, the French, under General Henri Navarre, could take no more. Attempting escape was even more deadly, as the Vietnamese were laying heavy fire on the airstrip that was transporting the troops away. The Viet Minh stormed the French garrison and shortly after, the French surrendered. Over 11,000 soldiers were taken captive that day, and many were later executed. Dien Bien Phu was a terrible loss for the already beleaguered French, and it was the final nail in French Indochina's coffin. At the 1954 Geneva Conference in Switzerland, the French agreed to leave all of their former territory in Indochina. The communists were recognized as the sovereign government, but only in

North Vietnam. Southern Vietnam became a separate state under Bao Dai of the Nguyen Dynasty.

Earlier in the war, the United States had unsurprisingly pledged to aid the French in their struggle against the communists as much as they could, and by 1954, there were already many American "advisors" present in the country to oversee military activity. Eisenhower's government feared that it would be only a matter of time before the north invaded to retake the south. Since the military infrastructure was already there for them, they quickly installed their own government apparatus. The Americans appointed the brutal dictator Ngo Dinh Diem as ruler, and South Vietnam turned into little more than an American puppet state. It became clear that the Americans simply had no intention of leaving the country, as the French had done, and were prepared to go to war if need be. Now, the stage was set for a massively increased American military presence and, ultimately, the beginning of the Vietnam War, a conflict that by the 1970s would enrage and utterly consume American culture itself. Before this happened, though, the Americans had already versed themselves in war in Asia, and the first time the Cold War turned "hot" was on a small peninsula some 3,000 kilometers from Vietnam.

CHAPTER 8:
AMERICA GOES TO WAR

The most remarkable feature of the Cold War between the USA and USSR was the fact that their two militaries never actually fought each other. This did not necessarily mean that the two did not have roles in funding and promoting opposing sides in wars, though, and from 1948 through the 1980s there were many "proxy wars." These conflicts, like the First Indochina War, were fought between two smaller powers yet represented the wider ideological battle between American capitalism and Soviet communism. No area of the earth saw more of these major conflicts than Asia. Asia is also the place where the Americans were most willing to actually send their young men to war.

Boots on the Ground: America and the Korean War

In August 1945, as WWII was quickly and violently drawing to a close, the Soviet Union turned their attention to Japan, a nation they had not yet officially declared war on. The Red Army focuses first on the Korean peninsula, an annex of Japan since 1910. The Soviets pushed aggressively into the peninsula and made rapid progress, which was another source of stress for the Americans, who feared that the Soviets might end up conquering all of Korea before Japan surrendered. After the atomic bombings of Nagasaki and Hiroshima had forced the

Japanese into submission, the Soviets halted their southward march, having reached the 38th parallel that runs through the peninsula. After reaching an agreement with the United States, this line became the new border between North and South Korea. After the war, the Soviets continued to occupy the North, while the Southern portion sort of fell into the lap of America. After all, such a small nation would be hard-pressed to remain independent for long with the Soviets so close by, and no other Western nation besides America was in any position to be able to support them (France, of course, had plenty of its own problems in Indochina). It was also not an option to simply give the southern portion back to Japan, considering the aggressive war they had waged and the fact that Japan itself was now occupied by Douglas MacArthur's forces.

As they did everywhere else, they gained control; the Soviets quickly installed a communist government in North Korea led by Kim Il-Sung. Stalin and later Mao were staunch supporters of the Kim government, while Kim's enemies in the South enjoyed the wholehearted assistance of the Americans and their allies. Syngman Rhee, an elderly Korean politician, became the American-sanctioned leader of the new state. Rhee quickly proved himself to be a brutal dictator who was ruthless in enforcing the new laws of South Korea and had no qualms about slaughtering his opponents. Regardless, the United States was always willing to "look the other way" when it came to supporting dictators and mass murderers, so long as they toed the line. Rhee, for his part, was a vehement anti-communist and was pro-American in all of his policy-making decisions. He led a bloody crusade against South Korean communists and actively persecuted those suspected of sympathizing with North Korea under the Kim government. In 1948, the southern Korean island of Jeju erupted in a revolt led by communists, and the Rhee government brutally put it down, ultimately resulting in thousands of civilian deaths, most of whom were not communists at all. The reaction to the Jeju revolt may have been useful in suppressing communism for a moment, but the extreme violence of the government actually led to a massive upswell of support and sympathy for North Korea. In the space of just a few years, southerners were already questioning whether a communist lifestyle truly was the best way forward.

It was clear that neither Rhee nor Kim were satisfied with the borders as they stood in 1945. Neither was willing to settle for only half of Korea, and the communist North was constantly being encouraged to expand by Joseph Stalin and was emboldened with military and financial support from the Soviets. In the years after the division of Korea, there was almost constant violence at the border, and Korean deaths numbered in the thousands in the years leading up to 1950. In 1949, Kim organized the creation of a special guerilla military force made up of communists and pro-North Koreans living in the South. Their goal was to weaken the South through clandestine military operations, and they proved quite successful early on. Thousands of North Korean soldiers soon began secretly crossing the border into the South under disguise to assist the guerilla armies there, and with their help, they began gaining significant ground.

For most of the 1940s, though, Stalin outright refused to give consent for a full-scale invasion. Both American and Soviet troops were present on the peninsula at the time, and with the backdrop of the Cold War, any open fighting could escalate rapidly and risk triggering a Third World War. By 1950, the situation was radically different. Soviet troops had been pulled out of the North in 1948, and the Americans followed suit the next year. A genuine invasion could now take place on the peninsula without the risk of Soviet troops confronting American ones. Plus, by 1949, the power differential between America and the USSR had been equalized. For 4 years, the United States had the ability to drop nuclear weapons on the USSR if they wanted to, and there would have been precious little Stalin could do about it. But in the summer of 1949, the success of the Soviet Union's inaugural atomic test entrenched them as a global nuclear superpower, capable of deadly retaliation in the event of an attack. Finally, the recent victory of Mao's Chinese communists meant that there was now a second large communist power able to provide support to the North Koreans. Just as the North Koreans contributed men and money to the CCP as they struggled in their revolution, the Chinese were now willing to lend a hand. In this environment, war was only a matter of time.

Stalin also wanted to use the Korean situation to test the limits of his adversary, Harry Truman. His administration had repeatedly refused to commit troops or provide military assistance to the KMT during the war against Mao, so why would they bother to interfere on behalf of the South Koreans? Stalin was still hesitant to commit troops, though, in the event that the Americans called their bluff. Instead, the Soviets directly assisted in planning the invasion, and they dispatched high-ranking military "advisors" to provide counsel for the North Korean forces. The stage was now set for a classic proxy war. The secret of the invasion was a surprisingly well-kept one—up to the very day of the invasion, very few Americans suspected an imminent invasion, and Truman and his entire administration were taken by surprise when the first border crossing occurred. As a last attempt to find a peaceful solution, Kim sent dignitaries to the South to negotiate an end to the border violence and, more importantly, to lobby for a Korea-wide election. A vote across the entire peninsula would result in the reunification of Korea, and the people themselves would be able to choose which government would rule them. Unsurprisingly, Rhee's response to the last hope for peace was a bitter refusal to hold a democratic election.

On June 25, less than a month after this breakdown of diplomacy, the communist Korean People's Army (KPA) launched their invasion into the South. The Southern military was notably corrupt and underequipped, and many South Korean soldiers defected to the communist side almost as soon as the fighting began. Being equipped with superior weaponry provided by the Chinese and Soviets, the KPA found much early success, and Syngman Rhee fled the southern capital of Seoul within days of the border crossing. On June 28, Seoul was captured, and in response, Rhee ordered the mass execution of any South Koreans even suspected of being communists. The goal was simply to kill as many of them as possible, and in what became known as the Bodo League Massacre, tens of thousands of South Korean civilians were slaughtered by their own government.

The Korean War had begun. Stalin had cast his die, and the ball was now firmly in Truman's court. Everyone's eyes were on America, and the world nervously waited to witness their response. At some point during the chaos, the Americans learned that Stalin had already committed himself to keeping troops out of Korea, and knowing that, it was relatively safe to intervene. Just five years after the conclusion of World War II, Truman and his cabinet felt that it was once again time for American boots on the ground. In order to garner support for the idea of sending even more young American men off to die in another foreign war, Truman hilariously compared the threat of North Korea to that of Nazi Germany:

> "We will continue to take every honorable step we can to avoid general war.... But we will not engage in appeasement. . .The world learned from Munich that security cannot be bought by appeasement" (AmericanForeignRelations.com).

Later, he commented:

> "I remembered how each time that the democracies failed to act, it had encouraged the aggressors to keep going ahead. Communism was acting in Korea just as Hitler, Mussolini and the Japanese had acted ten, fifteen and twenty years earlier.... If this was allowed to go unchallenged it would mean a third world war, just as similar incidents had brought on a second world war" (AmericanForeignRelations.com).

Kim Il-Sung was apparently the new Adolf Hitler, and with that, American troops prepared for deployment from nearby occupied Japan. On July 1st, the first American troops landed in South Korea, prepared to fight the Northern communists. Four days later, in the northern Gyeonggi Province, the Battle of Osan began, the first battle involving American troops. Unfortunately, the Americans were poorly equipped and even more poorly prepared for open conflict, and the KPA won a resounding victory. Casualties were comparably few, but several dozen American soldiers died, and dozens more were taken prisoner by the North. The KPA continued to make great strides in their southward invasion even despite the presence of American troops. By the beginning of September, Kim and the KPA were in control of nearly the entire Korean peninsula. The Americans only doubled down on the war. They began flooding South Korea with weapons, armored vehicles, and soldiers.

With this infusion of force, the situation quickly reversed, and the KPA was on the run. In mid-September, the Americans invaded Incheon, near Seoul, in northern South Korea. Seoul was retaken from the communists on the 25th, and the Americans threatened to cut off all the KPA's southern forces. To avoid being trapped in South Korea, they quickly retreated north toward the 38th parallel. Seoul would continue to change hands throughout the war, but for now, the South was secured, and they began pushing into North Korea. The KPA kept being pushed back, and in a complete reversal of the situation just weeks ago, the South Korean-American coalition was now in control of the majority of the peninsula. Then, as Southern victory approached in late 1950, the war took a shocking turn. As US forces approached Korea's border with China, Douglas MacArthur suggested that they push their luck a bit further. He wanted to carry the invasion across the border into China to topple the new CCP government but was rebuked by President Truman. In one of the most audacious moments of MacArthur's career, he even floated the idea of using nuclear weapons against both North Korea and China, a move that would have annihilated America's credibility as a defender of global freedom. Again, Truman shot this idea down.

For the most part, the Americans didn't consider an invasion of China because they didn't consider them to be a threat, despite China's repeated threats of intervening in Korea if they continued to press northward. American Generals did not take these warnings seriously, and when the Chinese finally joined the North Koreans in arms in October, Truman and his advisors were taken by surprise once again.

To their horror, *over one million* Chinese troops began pouring into North Korea, and in November, the first clashes between Americans and Chinese troops began. The Chinese-KPA alliance once again found much success and was able to push the Americans back out of the North by year's end. The war continued to rage for years, with back-and-forth territorial conquests around the border region. The border eventually more or less stabilized, and the war devolved into a stalemate, with skirmishes along the border becoming commonplace again. Several attempts were made at brokering peace, but success only came on July 27, 1953, after it became clear that total conquest of Korea would be costly for both sides. Even then, the two sides only agreed to halt hostilities, and no official peace deal was ever reached. To this day, North and South Korea have remained in a decades-long ceasefire, and the threat of war reigniting has never left the peninsula.

Mao, Ho Chi Minh, and the Vietnam War

The Korean War was an important turning point in Cold War politics. It was an important testing ground to see how far the US and USSR were willing to go, and the American public demonstrated their willingness to commit the lives of another generation of young men, all for the sake of containing a political ideology all the way across the Pacific Ocean. Clearly, as in Latin America, the US was also content to support dictators across the world so long as they suppressed communism. In Vietnam, though, America's boldness was pushed to its limit. After the Americans took over stewardship of southern Vietnam in place of the French, the Viet Minh continued their insurgent activities for years, but until 1957, Southern Vietnamese dictator Ngo Dinh Diem had mostly suppressed them. The year prior, Diem had begun rounding up, torturing, and executing all suspected communists in the South, just as Rhee did in Korea, and just like Rhee, Diem's popularity tanked as a result of the slaughters. He made some half-hearted attempts to correct this, most notably by introducing some limited land reform policies and allowing peasants to purchase land from large owners. This quickly fell through, though, as the majority of Diem's support came from the wealthiest large landowners in the country, who demanded he revert the policy.

In May 1957, Diem made a trip to the United States to meet with a delegation of Americans, including President Eisenhower. Because of his bloody repression of communists in the South, Diem was hailed as a Vietnamese hero by the government, and he was welcomed with a ticker-tape parade in his honor in New York City. Eisenhower personally fawned over him:

"President Ngo Dinh Diem stands for the highest qualities of heroism and statesmanship. The president of Vietnam, by his inspiring leadership, is opening up vast new areas for the peaceful progress of mankind" (Jacobs, 2006).

To the dismay of Eisenhower, the months following Diem's tour saw a string of victories for the Southern insurgents. They began a massive terror campaign that targeted both government officials and civilians. The Chau Doc Massacre on July 11, 1957, just two months after Diem's American visit, took the lives of nearly 20 patrons of a local bar. From late 1957 through 1958, the communists continued to gain traction through successful political attacks, despite civilian losses.

The situation in Vietnam has become far murkier in the years since 1953. That was the year of the so-called Sino-Soviet Split, where after Joseph Stalin died and Nikita Khrushchev became the Soviet leader, Mao denounced his attempts to remove Stalinist influence as blatant revisionism. Chinese-Soviet relations steadily worsened from then on, weakening the global communist alliance, but Ho Chi Minh was able to expertly pit the now-competing powers against each other to gain support for his own conflict. Further, after Diem unseated Emperor Bao in the South and refused to hold the elections that the 1954 Geneva Conference called for, Ho now had the most democratic credentials of any Vietnamese leader, which did wonders for his popular support. Still, the threat of American intervention was growing by the day, particularly after October 1957, when a Viet Minh-organized raid on the southern capital of Saigon wounded several American citizens there. In the event of American boots on the ground, it was unclear whether or not the USSR or China would be willing to work together to directly aid them.

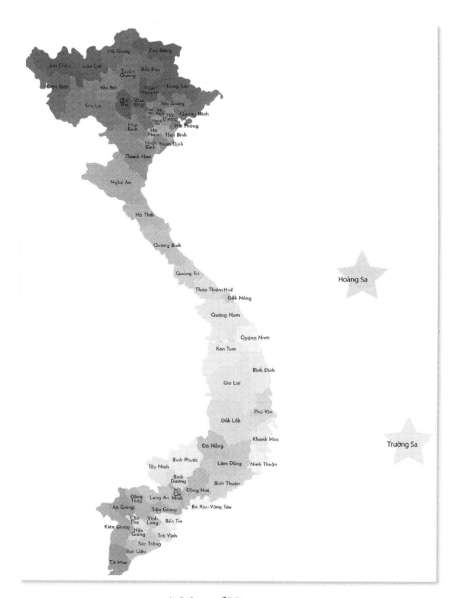

A Map of Vietnam.

In 1959, the Ho Chi Minh Trail was created by cutting a path through the dense jungles of neighboring Cambodia and Laos, through which soldiers and weapons were funneled into South Vietnam from the North. This provided cover and concealment for troop movements, and Diem was shocked at the inpouring of hostiles, seemingly from nowhere. Then, in 1960, the various rebel groups in the South were organized under the creation of the National Liberation Front, also known as the infamous Viet Cong (VC). The VC quickly garnered considerable public support as they called for the complete removal of American troops stationed there. Ho called for them to begin a massive revolt all across the South, and the communists captured large portions of the country. Meanwhile, Diem had done a full 360-turn on his promise of land reform and instead began forcibly taking land from peasants and returning it to the large landowners. The VC, on the other hand, was seizing land and distributing it to the peasants in the area, a move that caused support to swing wildly in the communists' favor.

In 1960, US presidential elections resulted in the rise of John F. Kennedy as president. By the next year, he was facing serious problems. First, there were about 1,000 American military personnel in South Vietnam, and the question remained what to do with them as the conflict raged. Pull them out and risk another communist victory. Or commit even more troops and risk more deaths? Second, the Berlin Wall had been erected by East Germany and the USSR, a massive blockade that bisected the city of Berlin in order to prevent Easterners from fleeing the West. This caused massive geopolitical tension for decades. Third, a far more dire threat was quickly emerging far closer to home, and it carried the threat of nuclear annihilation for a large portion of the United States. As we'll see, this last problem absolutely consumed JFK's political energy, but for now, he simply could not risk losing Vietnam.

An image of John F. Kennedy, the 35th American President.

JFK was hesitant to commit more troops to Vietnam, but given the political situation, he determined there was no alternative. And so, American involvement was ramped up massively, and within 2 years, there were over 15,000 American boots on the ground in Indochina. After all, the corrupt and massively incompetent Southern Vietnamese Army under Diem had no hope of winning on its own. Concerned with the VC's popularity among peasants, JFK in 1961–1962 promoted the "Hamlet Program," designed to isolate the VC from the poor. American and South Vietnamese forcibly relocated peasants from their communities to fortress-like villages constructed by the US to keep the VC out. Unsurprisingly, this was another wildly unpopular move and caused more resentment toward the Diem government and American presence. Plus, to the horror of the US, Diem seemed more concerned with persecuting his own people than winning the war. The CIA soon authorized a coup by the South Vietnamese against the government, which successfully led to Diem's overthrow and execution in 1963. US officials were ecstatic, but the assassination led to severe unrest in the South, and the government became incapable of accomplishing almost anything at all. JFK, though, would not live to see the results of his meddling in Vietnam, as just 20 days later, Kennedy himself was assassinated in Dallas. His Vice President, Lyndon Johnson, rose to power to finish his term, marking another turning point in the Vietnam War.

On August 2, 1964, the American ship USS Maddox fired upon several ships in the North Vietnamese Navy, which Ho had created in 1955. The Vietnamese returned fire, and a short skirmish ensued. The Americans under Johnson were looking for an excuse to be more aggressive with North Vietnam, and two days later, they got it. Another supposed communist attack on American ships happened, which became widely known as the Gulf of Tonkin incident. However, as it turns out, this second attack was almost certainly completely fabricated by American intelligence services, but at the time, this didn't matter. Most everyone saw it as a blatant act of aggression toward America, and by the time people started to question whether it really happened as the Americans said it did, it was too late. The die had been cast. Congress quickly passed the Gulf of Tonkin Resolution, which granted President Johnson increased executive power to intervene in opposition to communists in Vietnam. In short order, thousands upon thousands of American troops were being shipped off to Vietnam to wage a destructive and criminal war that would rage on for another decade, scarring an entire generation of American soldiers. The Gulf of Tonkin "incident" kicked off an unprecedented era of American involvement in the region and was a bloody reminder that the Cold War could turn hot at any moment. Continued escalation in Vietnam over the years was a foreboding sign of the future of the Cold War between the USA and USSR, but it could not compare to the terror they faced just a few years ago on a small island just miles away from the coast of southern Florida...

CONCLUSION:

THE EDGE OF ANNIHILATION—KENNEDY, KHRUSHCHEV, AND CASTRO'S NUCLEAR WEAPONS

Revolution in Cuba and the Bay of Pigs Invasion

In 1962, 17 years after the end of WWII and the beginning of the US-USSR global rivalry, the Cold War reached a terrifying climax. The US, USSR, and Cuba very nearly became embroiled in an international nuclear war, all because the United States could not bear the idea of a communist government so close to its borders. In 1953, the year before the US government toppled the Arbenz government in Guatemala, an armed revolution began in Cuba, another worrying development that threatened American control in Latin America. It began on July 26 with an attack on the Moncada Barracks in revolt against the brutal dictatorship of US-backed Fulgencio Batista, a murderous anti-communist who allowed American exploitation of his country. The attack on Moncada failed almost instantly, however, and the surviving rebels, including their leader, Fidel Castro, fled for Mexico.

The rebels worked to gather resources and support while in exile and were able to recruit some important people who became legendary figures in later years, including the Argentinian doctor Ernesto "Che" Guevara. In late 1956, Castro, Che, and the rebels re-entered Cuba but were almost completely destroyed upon landing by the Cuban Army. Again, the survivors fled, this time into the Sierra Maestra mountains, where they won huge support from the peasant population and Cuban workers. Che, who provided medical attention to the poor locals wherever they went, was instrumental in their rising popularity. The American government was distressed by Castro's fame, though the Cuban Revolution was not inherently a communist one. Che was a genuine communist and did much to inject communist ideology into the movement, but Castro repeatedly denied being a communist and rejected the idea of becoming a Soviet puppet. The movement was made up of a plurality of ideologies, including anarchism (Camilo Cienfuegos, one of Castro's top commanders, was a devoted anarchist), but the foremost of these was simply national liberation. In the context of the Cold War, however, there was simply no room for nuance. If you weren't aligned with the American economy, you were a communist fit for destruction.

Like other anti-communist dictators like Rhee and Diem, Batista, in 1958, began a bloody crackdown on suspected Castro supporters, while Castro led a massive offensive in the southern mountains to drive out the army. It was a massive success, and the armies of Castro and Che burst out of the Sierra Maestra as Cuban soldiers retreated to the north of the island. By December 1958, Batista was on the run, and Castro was closing in. That month, the rebels won their most decisive victory at the great Battle of Santa Clara. Che's army was able to capture thousands of soldiers, and a fortified supply train was filled with weapons and ammunition that the Army desperately needed. Within hours of the fall of Santa Clara, Batista fled Cuba.

On January 2, 1959, the armies of Che and Cienfuegos rolled into the capital, Havana, unopposed, and six days later, Castro entered the city, and the revolution came to a close. The Eisenhower administration immediately began drafting plans for an invasion of the island. Once again, the US began meddling in the affairs of a sovereign nation whose destiny the Americans had vowed to allow them to determine themselves. CIA Director Allen Dulles, who was heavily involved in the Guatemala coup, began recruiting Cuban exiles living in southern Florida and training them for combat. While this was going on, Eisenhower's second term was coming to an end, and both new presidential candidates, Richard Nixon and JFK, made the Cuban situation a focus of their campaigns, and both took an aggressive stance on Castro. After JFK's victory, he was briefed on the invasion plans by Eisenhower, and Kennedy ultimately gave the go-ahead. On April 17, 1961, transport ships filled with Cuban exiles and CIA officers landed in Cuba's Bay of Pigs. When Castro was awoken by the news, he immediately activated militia groups across the country, whom Che had warned for months to be ready for an invasion. The Americans had been operating under the assumption that Cubans at large did not support Castro, and the small invasion force would prompt Cubans everywhere to rise up against him, accomplishing the mission by themselves. This was a disastrous assumption, as Castro's popularity in these early years was incredibly high, and the result was an absolute rout of the invasion force. Over 1,000 men were captured within days, including some Americans who were later executed. Many of the captured Cubans were discovered to have actually been wanted men who had been charged with torture and murder by the Castro regime. These men were executed as well.

A map of the island shows that "Baia dei Porci" is where the
Bay of Pigs invasion took place, just south of Havana.

By April 20, the invasion had ended in a humiliating defeat, and the embarrassed Americans responded with an aggressive embargo of the country. The Americans also pressured all of their allies to cease all trade with Cuba, a small island nation that was now fully isolated. For the Cuban government, though, the American invasion was a great boon. They had lost no land, and the clear military aggression had proven the whole point of the Cuban Revolution. Castro had been arguing all along that the island functioned as little more than a tool for proppping up the American economy and as a casino and brothel for rich American politicians and businessmen. Support for Castro, which was already considerable by 1961, skyrocketed after the ill-fated coup. His government was now seen as a protector against exploitation and as a guarantor against foreign belligerence. Che acknowledged this much later, in August of that year, at the Inter-American Economic and Social Council convention in Uruguay. Kennedy advisor Richard Goodwin, who spoke with Che at the conference, later recalled:

> "He wanted to thank us very much for the invasion—that it had been a great political victory for them—enabled them to consolidate— and transformed them from an aggrieved little country to an equal" (from Jones, 2012).

Still, the Americans were a clear and present threat to Castro and his new regime. As it stood, Cuba was more alone than they had ever been before, and a strong ally would be needed if the Revolution was to survive. In the bipolar post-WWII world, Castro was faced with few options. America's blatant military aggression and embargo, ironically, drove Castro into the eager arms of Nikita Khrushchev and the USSR. Few countries in the world could afford to remain neutral in this political climate, and Cuba was no exception. With the likelihood of further American aggression, Castro, who had previously rejected the possibility of seeking Soviet support and alliances, was now steadily transforming his country into a communist state. This was a dramatic turning point in the history of the already tense relationship between the United States and Latin America.

The Cuban Missile Crisis

At the request of Castro, who feared further US invasion and believed that the next invasion would very likely involve the full might of the US army, the USSR began sending arms and military advisors to Cuba, as well as defensive weapons like surface-to-air missiles, to defend against bombing campaigns like the one that drove Arbenz into submission. Still, the ever-paranoid Castro feared it wouldn't be enough. In July 1962, Castro and Khrushchev held a meeting where they both agreed that nuclear deterrence was a necessity. So, the Soviets began transferring large amounts of rockets and nuclear warheads to Cuba, all of which were capable of striking America. Before the Americans discovered this, they were aware of the Soviet military buildup on the island, and they responded with harsh diplomatic appeals to the USSR, as well as military threats. On October 16, however, an American spy plane captured photographs showing the construction of missile silos in Cuba, and it was immediately clear that the USSR was preparing to arm America's neighbor with nuclear weapons.

Frankly, American officials were terrified, and the prospect of nuclear annihilation loomed large. Everyone agreed something had to be done, but needless to say, the situation required extreme delicacy. Many preferred a diplomatic solution. On October 18, Soviet Foreign Minister Andrei Gromyko met with President Kennedy to discuss the general tensions between Cuba and the US. Gromyko and the Soviet government were not yet aware that Kennedy knew of the missiles, and Kennedy chose not to confront him about it at that meeting. Gromyko's first order of business was to demand that America stop threatening Cuba, an irony that stunned Kennedy and his advisors. Gromyko insisted that all the weapons and equipment being sent to the Cuban military were solely for defensive purposes, to which the President later told the nation, "That statement was false" (Kennedy, 1999). For the time being, Kennedy allowed the Soviets to continue believing their operation was a secret while his administration searched for diplomatic solutions. Realistically, though, the clearest solution was by no means diplomatic.

Believing that the Soviets would likely refuse to remove the missiles willingly, many in the government were eager to simply invade Cuba again and destroy the sites themselves. An invasion force was prepared, and the plan was nearly executed, but new, vital intelligence soon came to light, revealing that the Soviets' build-up had progressed much further than they initially believed. Not only did the Soviets have over 40,000 troops present on the island, but the nuclear-equipped warheads were, in fact, already present and ready to be fired. This new revelation meant that if the US did invade and they took longer than a few days to accomplish all of their goals, there was a real chance that the Cubans would deploy their nukes toward large American cities across the southern states. Plus, an invasion would pit American troops against Soviet ones, very likely leading to a Third World War. As the sleepless president told his advisors:

"We are going to have to face the fact that, if we do invade, by the time we get to these sites, after a very bloody fight, they will be pointed at us. And we must further accept the possibility that when military hostilities first begin, those missiles will be fired" (Kennedy, 1999).

After accepting that the risk of triggering another global war was too great to accept, Kennedy decided that the best course of action was a swift and aggressive military blockade of Cuba to prevent more men and weapons from flooding the country. At sea, as Soviet ships attempted to pass the American military blockade to bring goods into Cuba, an open war between America and the USSR also nearly broke out. After the President took the time to brief the nation on the situation at hand, there was widespread panic as many believed America was on the brink of nuclear war. In JFK's words:

"Good evening, my fellow citizens: - This Government, as promised, has maintained the closest surveillance of the Soviet military buildup on the island of Cuba. Within the past week, unmistakable evidence has established the fact that a series of offensive missile sites is now in preparation on that imprisoned island. The purpose of these bases can be none other than to provide a nuclear strike capability against the Western Hemisphere... Additional sites not yet completed appear to be designed for intermediate range ballistic missiles capable of traveling more than twice as far-and thus capable of striking most of the major cities in the Western Hemisphere, ranging as far north as Hudson Bay, Canada, and as far south as Lima, Peru. In addition, jet bombers, capable of carrying nuclear weapons, are now being uncrated and assembled in Cuba, while the necessary air bases are being prepared" (Kennedy, October 22, 1962, from loveman.sdsu.edu).

He continued, making connections between the current situation and the state of the world before the outbreak of World War II:

"The 1930's taught us a clear lesson: aggressive conduct, if allowed to go unchecked and unchallenged, ultimately leads to war. This nation is opposed to war. We are also true to our word. Our unswerving objective, therefore, must be to prevent the use of these missiles against this or any other country, and to secure their withdrawal or elimination from the Western Hemisphere"(Kennedy, October 22, 1962, from loveman.sdsu.edu).

Across the world, in every country the US occupied, from Europe to Asia, American forces were put on high alert and advised to prepare for the potential of a Third World War. Indeed, this was the closest the world has ever come to nuclear war, but in reality, the placement of these weapons was not that brazen. The United States had placed several nuclear weapons within striking distance of the USSR, including in Italy and even in Turkey, the USSR's southern neighbor. Khrushchev viewed the Cuban situation as a good opportunity to equalize the power dynamic and prevent the USSR from being trapped in a kind of nuclear bubble. On October 26, Khrushchev penned a letter to President Kennedy pointing out the hypocrisy with which the United States accuses the USSR of aggression:

> ..."you have surrounded the Soviet Union with military bases, surrounded our allies with military bases, set up military bases literally around our country, and stationed your rocket weapons at them? This is no secret. High-placed American officials demonstratively declare this. Your rockets are stationed in Britain and in Italy and pointed at us. Your rockets are stationed in Turkey... Do you believe that you have the right to demand security for your country and the removal of such weapons that you qualify as offensive, while not recognizing this right for us?" (quoted in Kennedy, 1999).

Fear of war reached its height on October 27 when the spy plane flown by American Major Rudolf Anderson was shot out of the sky above Cuba by Cuban and Soviet anti-air weapons. Anderson was killed in the resulting crash, much to the horror and sorrow of Kennedy's administration. The surface-to-air missiles that the Cubans now possessed posed a considerable threat to American airmen, and the death of Major Anderson was a foreboding sign of things to come. The entire world now held their breath, awaiting news that war between the Americans and Soviets was underway.

In the end, though, cooler heads prevailed, and ultimately, it was Soviet outreach that disarmed the crisis. Khrushchev made repeated overtures to Kennedy and begged him to consider the fact that a nuclear war would be a global calamity. He offered to withdraw all nuclear missiles in exchange for Kennedy's word that the US would never again invade Cuba. On October 28, Kennedy agreed to these terms, along with the Soviet request to remove all American nukes from Turkey (this condition was kept secret from the American public, however, so Kennedy could claim the resolution as an unambiguous American victory). Soviet troops began their journey back to the USSR, and Cuba was stripped of its nuclear capabilities. The threat of American invasion was at least over, and with that, the Cuban Missile Crisis wound to a close. Both American and Soviet leaders now had a lot of reflection to do after waltzing toward the very edge of global nuclear annihilation. The Cold War had reached a climax of anxiety, and for the first time in American history, the utter destruction of the nation seemed possible, even likely.

Such was the state of the world in the 20 tension-gripped years following the end of the Second World War. A world consumed with fear, paranoia, and enmity. The fall of the German Reich and the great old empires of Europe only ushered in the age of new, more frightening colossuses. The Americans and Soviets held their proxy wars and worked to create a future for the world in which they, and they alone, would guide destiny's hand. From the ashes of fascism rose another era of competing ideologies, an era of nuclear anxiety, and an era of endless global conflicts inevitably tied to the egos of the leaders of the world's two superpowers. The Cold War raged on for decades to come, infusing itself into every aspect of American and Soviet culture. Remnants of the conflict still affect the world today, in places like Cuba and North Korea, and even in America, where accusations of communism are still a convenient way to discredit those calling for social change. After the eventual demise of the bloated and corrupt Soviet government in the 1990s, America became the only global juggernaut. Its military superiority and cultural weight, which largely came as a result of the Second World War, still endure to this day, long after Cuba, long after Vietnam and East Germany, and long after the end of the Cold War.

REFERENCES

August 6, 1945: Statement by the President announcing the use of the A-bomb at Hiroshima. (n.d.). Miller Center. https://millercenter. org/the-presidency/presidential-speeches/august-6-1945-statement-president-announcing-use-bomb

Balfour declaration 1917. (n.d.) Yale Law School. https://avalon.law. yale.edu/20th_century/balfour.asp

British give date for Indian independence, 1947. UPI Archives. https:// www.upi.com/Archives/1947/02/20/British-give-date-for-Indian-independence/3317410585124/

Carlton, D. (2001). "Churchill and the two 'evil empires.'" *Transactions of the Royal Historical Society 11*, 331-351. https:// millercenter.org/the-presidency/presidential-speeches/august-6-1945-statement-president-announcing-use-bomb

Chomsky, N. (1969). *At war with Asia: Essays on Indochina.* Pantheon Books.

Coining a word and championing a cause: The story of Raphael Lempkin. (n.d.). US Holocaust Memorial Museum. https:// encyclopedia.ushmm.org/content/en/article/coining-a-word-and-championing-a-cause-the-story-of-raphael-lemkin

Cuban missile crisis address. (n.d.). San Diego State University. https://loveman.sdsu.edu/docs/1962Kennedy_missilecrisisspeech.pdf

DeGroot, G. (2004). *The bomb: A life.* Harvard University Press.

Digest of decisions and announcements: Important speeches by the Prime Minister. (n.d.). PM Transcripts. https://pmtranscripts.pmc.gov.au/sites/default/files/original/00000003_3.pdf

Fullbrook, M. (2014). *The divided nation: A history of Germany 1918-2014.* Wiley Blackwell.

Futamura, M. (2008). *War crimes tribunals and transitional justice: The Tokyo Trial and the Nuremberg legacy.* Routledge.

Gonzalez, S. (2002). *The nuclear deception: Nikita Khrushchev and the Cuban missile crisis.* Spooks Books.

Grada, C. (2019). *The famines of WWII.* Cepr.org. https://cepr.org/voxeu/columns/famines-wwii

Heale, M.J. (1998). *McCarthy's Americans: Red Scare politics in state and nation, 1935-1965.* Macmillan Press, Ltd.

Hogan, M. (1987). *The marshall plan: America, Britain, and the reconstruction of Western Europe, 1947-1952.* Cambridge: Cambridge University Press.

'Iron curtain' speech. (n.d.). nationalarchives.gov.uk. https://www.nationalarchives.gov.uk/education/resources/cold-war-on-file/iron-curtain-speech/

Jacobs, S. (2006). *Cold war Mandarin: Ngo Dinh Diem and the origins of America's war in Vietnam, 1950-1963.* Rowman and Littlefield Publishers.

Jacobsen, A. (2014). *Operation paperclip: The secret intelligence program that brought nazi scientists to America.* Little, Brown, and Company.

Jian, C. (1994). *China's Road to the Korean War*. Colombia University Press.

Judd, D. (2005). *The lion and the tiger: The rise and fall of the British Raj*. Oxford University Press.

Karsh, E. (2002). *The Arab-Israeli conflict: The Palestine war 1948*. Osprey Publishing.

Kennedy, R.F. (1999). *Thirteen days: A memoir of the Cuban missile crisis*. W. W. Norton and Company.

Malik, K. (2020). *Don't let the victors define morality – Hiroshima was always indefensible*. The Guardian. https://www.theguardian.com/commentisfree/2020/aug/09/dont-let-the-victors-define-morality-hiroshima-was-always-indefensible

Massad, J. (2006). *The persistence of the Palestinian question: Essays on Zionism and the Palestinians*. Routledge.

Mcmahon, RJ. (2021). *The cold war: A very short introduction*. London: Oxford University Press.

Medoff, R. (2009). *Blowing the whistle on genocide: Josiah E. Dubois Jr., and the struggle for a US response to the Holocaust*. Purdue University Press.

Moyar, M. (2006). *Triumph forsaken: The Vietnam war, 1954-1965*. Cambridge University Press.

Number of United States Military Personnel in Europe from 1950 to 2021. (2023, December 5). Statista Research Department. https://www.statista.com/statistics/1294309/us-troops-europe/#:~:text=Number%20of%20U.S.%20military%20personnel%20in%20Europe%201950%2D2021&text=The%20number%20of%20United%20States,1989%2C%20to%20107%2C158%20by%201995.

Opening statement before the international military tribunal. Robert H. Jackson Center. https://www.roberthjackson.org/speech-and-writing/

opening-statement-before-the-international-military-tribunal/

Perez-Stable, M. (1998). *The Cuban revolution: Origins, course, and legacy.* Oxford University Press.

Pruitt, S. (2023). *The post world war II boom: How America got into gear.* History.com. https://www.history.com/news/post-world-war-ii-boom-economy

Schlesinger, S. and Kinzer, S. (2005). *Bitter fruit: The story of the American coup in Guatemala.* David Rockefeller Center for Latin American Studies.

The Marshall Plan Speech. The Marshall Foundation. https://www.marshallfoundation.org/the-marshall-plan/speech/

The Post War World. (n.d.). International Monetary Fund. https://www.imf.org/external/np/exr/center/mm/eng/mm_dr_01.htm

Tokyo War Crimes Trial. (n.d.). National WW2 Museum. https://www.nationalww2museum.org/war/topics/tokyo-war-crimes-trial

Truman's Loyalty Program. (n.d.). Truman Library. https://www.trumanlibrary.gov/education/presidential-inquiries/trumans-loyalty-program

Urofsky, M. (1995). *American Zionism from Herzl to the Holocaust.* Bison Books.

Vergun, D. (n.d.). *During WW2, industries transitioned from peacetime to wartime production.* US Department of Defense. https://www.defense.gov/News/Feature-Stories/story/article/2128446/during-wwii-industries-transitioned-from-peacetime-to-wartime-production/

Windrow, M. and Chappell, M. (1998). *The French-Indochina war, 1946-54.* Osprey Publishing.

Wood, A. (2007). *Holocaust: The events and their impact on real people.* DK Publishing.

IMAGES

1343024. (2016, April 28). *China map* [Image]. Pixabay. https://pixabay.com/illustrations/china-map-chinese-world-globe-1356803/

lotusarise. (2023, September 22). *India map* [Image]. Pixabay. https://pixabay.com/illustrations/india-map-india-indian-states-8268866/

OpenClipart-Vectors. (2013, October 10). *Israel Jewish* [Image]. Pixabay. https://pixabay.com/vectors/israel-jewish-palestine-palestinian-159602/

U_89885r2vy0. (2013, January 2). *Mushroom cloud atomic bomb* [Image]. Pixabay. https://pixabay.com/photos/mushroom-cloud-atomic-bomb-67534/

uwebeierbergen. (2015, January 21). *Map Germany* [Image]. Pixabay. https://pixabay.com/vectors/map-germany-federal-states-606538/

WikiImages. (2013, January 2). *Mushroom cloud atomic bomb* [Image]. Pixabay. https://pixabay.com/photos/mushroom-cloud-atomic-bomb-67534/

WikiImages. (2012, December 20). *John F. Kennedy president* [Image]. Pixabay. https://pixabay.com/photos/john-f-kennedy-president-usa-63160/

WikiImages. (2012, December 4). *Stamp shaking hands* [Image]. Pixabay. https://pixabay.com/photos/stamp-shaking-hands-handshake-62921/

WikimediaImages. (2015, August 22). *Bay of Pigs Cuba* [Image]. Pixabay. https://pixabay.com/vectors/bay-of-pigs-cuba-map-geography-895018/

Made in the USA
Columbia, SC
01 December 2024

c7a95233-2520-4e8a-b265-3762397ae059R01